INVASION OF THE PARTY SNATCHERS

How the Holy-Rollers and Neo-Cons Destroyed the GOP

VICTOR GOLD

SOURCEBOOKS, INC.®
NAPERVILLE, ILLINOIS

Published by Sourcebooks, Inc.
P.O. Box 4410, Naperville, Illinois 60567-4410
(630) 961-3900
Fax: (630) 961-2168
www.sourcebooks.com

Printed and bound in the United States of America.
LB 10 9 8 7 6 5 4 3 2

To Lyn Nofziger and Paul Wagner

VIVA! OLÉ!

CONTENTS

Reader's Advisory vii

Chapter 1   Where Do Elephants Go to Die? 1

Chapter 2   The Pat and Jerry Show 17

Chapter 3   Newt and the Destroyers:
             Enter the 104th Congress 35

Chapter 4   Like Father, Unlike Son 55

Chapter 5   The Imperial Vice Presidency 79

Chapter 6   A Leaf Flew in the Window 99

Chapter 7   The Coulterization of
             Republican Rhetoric 117

Chapter 8   Their Eyes Have Seen the Glory
             (The Theo-Con Agenda) 139

Chapter 9   The K Street Caper 155

Chapter 10 Harding Was a Piker 165

Chapter 11 Clinton Redux: Symbols
             and Sideshows 179

Chapter 12 The Sinclair Lewis Presidency 191

Chapter 13 What Would Barry Do? 205

Chapter 14 The Great Divide 223

Index 237

READER'S ADVISORY

Neo-Cons: Abbreviation for Neo-Conservatives; aka Kristolites, after their ideological mentor, Irving Kristol. A quarter-century-old political movement made up of a willing coalition of disillusioned Kennedy-Johnson Democrats, smarter-than-thou Eastern intellectuals, and unregenerate Wilsonian imperialists.

Theo-Cons: Abbreviation for Theocrat-Conservatives; aka True Believers, Holy Rollers. A quarter-century-old political movement made up of a sanctimonious coalition of disillusioned Jimmy Carter Democrats, holier-than-thou televangelists, and unregenerate anti-Darwinians.

GOP: Abbreviation for Grand Old Party; aka the Republican Party (*see also* Elephant). A major American political movement once characterized by secular conservative policies favoring decentralized federal government, free-market economics, fiscal restraint, and a restrictive view of presidential power to commit American lives and resources to foreign military ventures. Born Ripon, WI, 1856; died Washington, D.C., circa 2001–2006 (though a party by that name, principally operated by Neo-Cons and Theo-Cons, continues to appear on the ballots of fifty states and the District of Columbia).

"The great danger in the new conservative movement is that instead of broadening its base, the movement might tear itself and the GOP apart."

—Barry Goldwater, 1988

(as usual, twenty years ahead of his time)

Chapter 1

WHERE DO ELEPHANTS GO TO DIE?

"Sometimes party loyalty asks too much."
—JOHN F. KENNEDY, ON REFUSING TO NOMINATE
A DEMOCRAT HE DISLIKED TO A JUDGESHIP (1961)

NOVEMBER 7, 2006 (5 minutes to midnight): You know something has gone wrong in your political universe when the party you've worked and voted with for over forty years is getting blown out in a national election and you feel good about it.

Election Night Flashbacks:
   November 2, 1994: Twelve years before, I'd been at an election night party at Dick and Lynne Cheney's home in

1

McLean, Virginia, cheering the Republican landslide that swept a corrupt, self-aggrandizing Democratic majority out of power on Capitol Hill. Some called it "the Gingrich revolution," though the new Speaker of the House had nothing to do with a GOP sweep that included George W. Bush's unexpected victory over Ann Richards in Texas and George Pataki's upset win over Mario Cuomo in New York.

November 7, 2000: *Six years later, I'd celebrated the news that a cascade of ballots coming out of south Florida had carried the state and the election for the Bush-Cheney ticket. Premature cheering as it developed, but Al Gore's concession speech a month later cleared the way for the first Republican takeover of both the White House and the Congress in nearly half a century.*

Separately and together, those were the election night returns conservative Republicans had been waiting for since the Goldwater presidential campaign of 1964: Big Government Liberalism repudiated, Republicans in control at both ends of Pennsylvania avenue, from Congress to the White House.

Yet, there I was on election night 2006, an aging Goldwater conservative who felt not only good but also gratified that all this was unraveling state by state and district by district. A Democratic landslide was sweeping a corrupt, self-aggrandizing Republican congressional majority out of power and, hard as they tried, the disingenuous party hacks spouting the White House line on Fox News couldn't explain it away. What came to mind watching these Beltway blowhards was an old Joe South lyric from the 1970s: "These are not my people."

Indeed, there was little I saw or heard from any of the Republican leaders and spokesmen after the 2006 midterm elections that reflected the party I'd joined as a young activist forty years before. What I saw instead was a party of pork-barrel ear-markers like Dennis Hastert, of political hatchet men like Karl Rove, and of Bible-thumping hypocrites like Tom DeLay, all giving oleaginous cover to a profligate Congress that ran up eye-popping deficits and an insulated White House run by a self-righteous Texan and his arrogant inner circle of sycophants and cronies.

In short, everything in government that repelled me about the Democratic party of Lyndon Johnson when I left it to join a nascent conservative movement in Barry Goldwater's presidential campaign of 1964. And the thought ran through my mind, *What would Barry say if he were alive?*

Barry Goldwater: A straight-talking, freethinking maverick from Arizona, the political godfather of modern American conservatism. But wait ...

For those Generation-X , -Y, and -Z activists whose knowledge of political history is limited to what they hear on talk radio and scan on the Internet, a proper conservative introduction is in order. Here's what one of Barry's harshest critics four decades back more recently said of him:

"No democracy can survive if it is wormy with lies and evasions. That is why we must cherish those people who have the guts to speak the truth: mavericks, whistle-blowers, disturbers

of the public peace. And it's why, in spite of my own continuing (though chastened) liberal faith, I miss Barry Goldwater. More than ever."

—PETE HAMILL, *LOS ANGELES TIMES*, AUGUST 16, 2004

Lies and *evasions*: No two words could better describe the modus operandi of the Bush-Cheney administration and today's Republican party, masquerading as "conservative" in the Goldwater tradition.

Pause again to define "conservative" as young activists who joined the 1964 Goldwater campaign understood the term:

- In foreign policy, though he broke with the isolationism of pre–World War II Republicans, Goldwater rejected the Wilsonian notion—now advanced by the Neo-Cons and their evangelical allies—that America has a God-given mission to shape the world in its image.

- In domestic policy, though a champion of free-market economics, Goldwater was a Western conservationist who rejected the laissez-faire notion— now advanced by the Halliburton arm of the Bush-Cheney White House—that what's good for corporate profits is necessarily good for the country.

- In cultural policy, though a Middle American moralist, Goldwater rejected the notion—now advanced by the "faith-based" branch of the Bush White House—that Big Brother in Washington has not only the right but the moral obligation to intrude into private relationships. ("Every good Christian," Barry once told an audience of reporters, "ought to give Jerry Falwell a swift kick in the ass.")

And more: Though a hard-line conservative, Goldwater spoke out forcefully against the Orwellian notion—now advanced by the Alberto Gonzales wing of the Bush-Cheney administration—that under the rubric of "national security" an imperial White House can run constitutional rights through a shredder.

That was the Barry Goldwater I worked for in 1964, the Goldwater even his critics came to understand and respect in the years that followed. What would he say about today's Republican party? How would he feel, if still in the U.S. Senate, about the Bush-Cheney White House that governs in the name of conservatism?

My hunch, as one of the last living Goldwaterites, is it would be something along the line of what he had to say about Jerry Falwell.

✶ ✶ ✶

"Politics is like bullfighting," Barry Goldwater once told me. "Getting gored is a risk you take."

The occasion was a bittersweet post-election staff party held not long after his landslide defeat in November 1964. Bitter because not enough time had passed to heal the wound; sweet because, bad as the beating was, the young conservatives in the crowd felt we'd started something.

And we had. A decade and a half later, Ronald Reagan, the rising political star of that campaign, would win the presidency in a landslide that changed the course of American politics.

Goldwater and Reagan

Odd company for someone who had cast his first vote for Adlai Stevenson in 1952 and supported John F. Kennedy in 1960. Odd but not singular: Like Reagan, I was one of thousands of disillusioned Democrats who made the switch to the party of Lincoln in 1964. Early Neo-Cons, you might call us. But unlike the Neo-Cons of today—the transient ex-Democrats who, in the words of their ideological Dalai Lama, Irving Kristol, were "mugged by reality"—we didn't switch with the idea in mind of reshaping the Republican party in our own image.

The "reality" that Kristol and other latter-day Neo-Cons claim they were mugged by was Liberalism's failure to deliver on its promise of universal peace and utopian plenty in a Great Society. A valid claim as far as it went, but the uglier reality they couldn't deal with was their loss of power and influence in the Democratic party. As old-line Kennedy-Johnson Democrats, Kristol, Bill Bennett, and their ideological soul mates had watched their last political hope, Henry "Scoop" Jackson, get crushed in the Democratic presidential primaries as first George McGovern's New Left radicals, then Jimmy Carter's "born-again" populists took over the party in the turbulent '70s. Foreign policy hawks as well as political opportunists, they had no problem crossing over to join the ranks of a resurgent Republican party headed by Ronald Reagan.

Correction: Not to join, but rather to *lead* the ranks. With the insufferable arrogance of an Eastern-seaboard intellectual lecturing what he perceived to be land-grant college yahoos, Kristol, in a blustering polemic titled "The Stupid Party," announced the Neo-Con mission as one of converting Republicans and American conservatives, *"against their respective wills,* into a new kind of conservative politics suitable to governing a modern democracy" (emphasis added).

No, *arrogance* doesn't quite nail it. The Greeks had a better word, *hubris.* And my grandfather, Sam the Tailor, a better word yet—*chutzpah.*

But why should any of this surprise us? Nothing so defines the bone-deep ideologue as his or her conviction that when things don't go the way they're supposed to— Five-Year Plans, Great Societies, Iraq wars—it isn't the *theory* that's flawed, only the way it was implemented.

So it is that six years into the country's first Neo-Con administration, what Americans have learned about Irving Kristol's "new kind of conservative politics" is that it's merely a recycled model of the old Liberal politics that led to the decline-and-fall of the Democratic party in the 1960s: a fiscally irresponsible, ever-expanding federal government presided over by an imperial executive imbued with a messianic view of America's right to "democratize" the heathen; or as Irving's Neo-Con son William, editor of the *Weekly Standard,* prefers, our moral duty to "actively pursue" policies leading to Woodrow Wilson's dream of a "benevolent global hegemony."

Translated from the Neo-Con: *Today we own Washington, tomorrow the world.*

Memory tracks to the story told in the mid-'70s about New York Mayor Ed Koch's investing a new municipal judge who'd been mugged by a street gang the night before. No matter, said the Mayor: the judge had assured him that he wouldn't let the incident cloud his thinking when police brought alleged perpetrators before the bench; to which someone in the audience—no doubt a member of the Stupid Party—called out, "Then mug 'im again!"

✳ ✳ ✳

The first rule of Hollywood, according to screenwriter William Goldman, is that "Nobody knows anything." Not so in Washington where, even before the Neo-Cons arrived, everybody claimed to know everything.

For those of us unhappy with the direction the country was headed in the mid-'60s, a large part of Barry Goldwater's appeal lay in his poor standing among the know-it-alls. What Pete Hamill now sees as Goldwater's refreshing candor was then viewed by his critics—Hamill included—as the frothing of a Sunbelt yahoo applying "simplistic" answers to "complex" questions.

Conceded, Goldwater's answers could sometimes be a spin doctor's nightmare and an opponent's delight. As his deputy press secretary during the '64 campaign, I could have lived with a more politic answer to a Knoxville reporter's question about what he'd do with the Tennessee Valley Authority if he became President Goldwater: "Sell it!" And where a Nixon might allude to weapons of "reduced collateral damage," no one but Barry would speak of missiles so accurate they could "hit the men's room in the Kremlin."

Simplistic, yes. On the other hand, what had the "complex" thinkers who made up the Washington establishment at the time—the Bundys, McCones, Cliffords, and Rostows—brought us? An escalating war in Southeast Asia with no apparent exit strategy, a breakdown in U.S. relations with its allies, the loss of American prestige and influence around the world...

Wait, there's more to the parallel: A posturing Texan in the Oval Office, a fork-tongued technocrat running the Pentagon (who in time would get booted), a Congress filled with tunnel-visioned members interested only in their own reelection in a town infested with influence-peddling lobbyists.

Not to forget the furrow-browed best-and-brightest—Robert McNamara's Whiz Kids in the '60s, Paul Wolfowitz's Vulcans forty years later—salivating to put their complex theories to the global test. And if those theories didn't work in the real world? If, instead of being greeted as liberators by the Vietnamese/Iraqis, thousands of young Americans were caught in the crossfire of a bloody civil war?

Good question, as the fatuous defenders of White House policy like to say on talk shows that fill our TV screens on Sunday mornings. In the 1960s, we had

Barry Goldwater to blow the whistle on their lies and evasions. Who's around to do it today? Bill O'Reilly and Matt Drudge?

$$* * *$$

"Get Off Clinton's Back"

The last time I saw Barry Goldwater he was in mid-campaign form, disturbing the public peace with contrarian comments about everything from gays in the military ("If they can shoot straight, what's the problem?") to Newt Gingrich's verbal diarrhea ("Can't anybody shut that guy up?").

The season was mid-summer, 1995. The occasion, a reunion of friends and former staffers from his 1964 presidential campaign—three decades past and ancient history, which made it all the more appropriate that we'd gather at the Jockey Club in Washington's Fairfax hotel, a faded relic of the Kennedy-Johnson '60s.

Goldwater had long since retired from the U.S. Senate but stayed in touch with things political through former colleagues on Capitol Hill. Like all Republicans who had served in Congress during the wilderness years of Democratic control, he relished his party's takeover of both houses of Congress in 1994. But maverick that he was, Barry soon fell out with the Gingrich-led House majority over the way it was handling its newfound power.

A year earlier, Goldwater had angered many of his fellow Republicans in Congress by urging them to "get off Clinton's back" and "let him be president." Typically, he didn't stop there: From all he'd heard about the ongoing Whitewater investigation, he told reporters, it wasn't "that big a deal."

Party-liners were aghast, but when the subject of Clinton and Whitewater came up at our Jockey Club reunion, Barry hadn't budged an inch. Whitewater, he allowed, was nothing more than a pissant Arkansas real estate deal. Before condemning it, he'd have to see a smoking gun that showed something illegal took place. Clinton, like every Liberal president Goldwater knew, was open to criticism ("He doesn't know a goddamned thing about foreign policy."), but only on "solid grounds"—issues that would play into the 1996 election, when Republicans had a good chance to retake the presidency.

It was at that point that the old maverick's concerns about what the media were calling "the Gingrich revolution" entered into our conversation. Contrary to his opponents' depiction of Goldwater as an intellectual lightweight, Barry was a keen student of political history. He remembered what had happened when Republicans won control of Congress in 1946, and then proceeded under erratic, tunnel-visioned leadership to be out-maneuvered and outwitted by an underrated Democratic president.

Goldwater's fear was that the Gingrich-led 104th Congress was headed down the same political path and that whoever won the GOP presidential nomination in 1996 would have to run, as did Thomas Dewey in 1948, weighed down by the record of an unpopular Congress. For Republicans of Goldwater's generation, the memory of Harry Truman's comeback, running not so much against Dewey as against "that good-for-nothing Republican Congress," remained very much alive.

Not that Newt Gingrich and his coterie of Hathaway-shirted "revolutionaries" would necessarily view a repetition of the 1948 debacle in the 1996 presidential election as a setback. On a personal level—and to Gingrich all politics was (and a decade later, remains) personal—a Republican White House in January 1997 would have relegated the Speaker of the House to the second tier of party leadership: No more top-of-the-news press conferences. (A running joke in those years was "The most dangerous place to stand on Capitol Hill is between Newt Gingrich and a TV camera.") It would have deprived the Speaker of the central role he knew God had given him in his ongoing struggle not only to reduce the size of federal bureaucracy but to save Western civilization from a second Dark Age.

But more yet: As Grover Norquist, the Speaker's Harvard-spawned ideological guru, put it shortly after the GOP took control of Congress, "The presidency is irrelevant." Meaning? That the new Republican congressional majority had all the power it needed to shrink the size of federal government, in Norquist's pithy phrase, "until it's small enough to drown in the bathtub."

This was all the reassurance that Newt, Tom DeLay, and other Republican leaders of the 104th needed to go to war against what they perceived as a wounded Clinton presidency. The battleground would be the shaping of the annual budget and the result—as Goldwater had perceived—would be a revival of Bill Clinton's political fortunes and a critical setback for the Republican party's hope of winning the presidency in 1996.

But worse was yet to come: Having failed to end Bill Clinton's political career at the polls, a fundamentalist Republican Congress, with DeLay at the whip, would pervert Goldwater's (as well as Ronald Reagan's) conservative legacy into a Hypocrites' Crusade to remove a sitting president for the high crime of violating the Seventh Commandment (and not telling his wife or the apostle Kenneth Starr about it).

And still worse would arrive in the year 2000 when, having reached the mountaintop—the election of both a Republican White House and Republican Congress—the party that called itself conservative proceeded, *Animal Farm*-like, to emerge as a party of Big Government, fiscal irresponsibility, and an executive branch that outdid even Lyndon Johnson in its imperial view of presidential power.

All that lay ahead, however, as we savored our Maryland crab cakes and shared memories of the distant political past in what would be Barry Goldwater's last Washington reunion with his old campaign staff: *gays in the military, stop picking on Clinton*...Barry had, as Bill Buckley once put it, "an inclination to keep his listeners on their toes."

Had Goldwater changed? Not a bit. To the day he died in May 1998, Barry remained the man Pete Hamill remembers as one of "those people who have the guts to speak the truth: mavericks, whistle-blowers, disturbers of the public peace." If anything had changed in the twilight of the old maverick's life, it was the party he and Ronald Reagan shaped into a vehicle for conservative governance in the last half of the 20th century.

* * *

"Where do elephants go to die?"

—LINE OVERHEARD BY THEODORE WHITE AT THE

REPUBLICAN GOVERNORS' CONFERENCE IN CLEVELAND, JUNE 1964

It was a line given added resonance later in the year, following Barry Goldwater's resounding defeat in the 1964 presidential election. With predictions that his party would soon go the way of Henry Clay's Whigs, even Dean Burch, the GOP National Committee chairman, was heard to say, "It's not a question of *whither* the Republican party but *whether* the Republican party."

As a matter of history, it wasn't the first time the party had been killed off by political prophets. When William Howard Taft, an incumbent Republican president, ran third in the three-man race for the White House in 1912, experts at the time predicted that Teddy Roosevelt's new-born Progressive movement would replace the GOP as America's second major party. And no less a prophet than historian Arthur Schlesinger, Sr., wrote the Republicans out of history in the Depression Thirties, a period when Franklin Roosevelt, in a triumphalist moment, played with the idea of reordering the country's party system along Liberal-Conservative lines (with Conservatives, needless to add, marginalized). Then, of course, there was Watergate and the dismal 1970s, a decade when Republican fortunes sank so low that a splintered Democratic party was able to win the presidency running a little-known Southern governor with a penchant for cosmic moralizing.

In each of these cases, come electoral disaster or White House scandal, the party proved more resilient than the prophets imagined. What went unforeseen, however, was that the elephant would at some point in the last years of the 20th century be possessed, in both body and spirit, by a coincident fusion of mutant ex-Liberals and holy-rolling Theocrats masquerading as conservatives in the tradition of Barry Goldwater and Ronald Reagan: Death by transmogrification, beginning with...

The Invasion of the Party Snatchers: Flashback to Detroit, July 1980...

Chapter 2

THE PAT AND JERRY SHOW

People walkin' up to ya,
Singin' "Glory Hallelujah"
An' they try to sock it to ya
In the name of the Lord.

—JOE SOUTH, "THE GAMES PEOPLE PLAY"

"NOT A BAD WEEK. Struck a well and the old man gets nominated vice president."

That was my introduction to the irreverent, yet-to-be-reborn George W. Bush who showed up at the Pontchartrain Hotel in Detroit the last day of the Republican national convention in July 1980. It was the Dubya—then known as "Junior"—whom I, along with

17

other members of his father's staff, would come to know and work with in those years: a laid-back thirty-something Texas oilman with a ready wit and facile tongue that would sometimes light up a press room.

Texas legend has it that only a few years later Karl Rove took one look at the oldest of the Bush sons and saw a political zircon in the making, raw material to be shaped by a master's hand for big things in Austin and beyond. If so, Rove is indeed the sagebrush Machiavelli he's reputed to be: Nothing, save an earthy affability and his family name, suggested the possibility that George W. might rise above the political level of a short-term west Texas congressman (if he could get that far). If there was a future governor in the family, Bush staffers agreed, it had to be second son Jeb, an impressive stump speaker (in fluent Spanish as well as panhandle-Florida English) with a wonkish passion for government as well as politics.

Young George had arrived at the convention after the late night in-fighting that would shape his father's and his own political future was over. I'd been with the Bushes the night before, while a cabal led by Henry Kissinger and Donald Rumsfeld was plotting feverishly a few blocks away to make their old White House boss Gerald Ford the vice presidential nominee on a "Dream Ticket" headed by Ronald Reagan.[1]

The plot would fail, but had the "Dream Ticket" worked out, it would have been no less than the third time

---

[1] Other ex-Ford satellites, including pollster Bob Teeter, were in on the plot, but, interestingly enough, not Rummy's old White House sidekick Dick Cheney. It was a calculated decision on Cheney's part that would serve him well in the years to come.

Rumsfeld had screwed George W.'s old man out of the vice presidency. The first occurred when Rumsfeld, as White House chief of staff, had urged Gerald Ford to nominate Nelson Rockefeller to the vice presidency in 1974, despite the fact that members of the Republican National Committee had overwhelmingly recommended Bush. The second occurred when Ford, with Rumsfeld again pulling the strings, named Bob Dole as his 1976 running mate, despite polls that showed Bush would have added more to the ticket.

Not to forget Rumsfeld's devious hand in persuading Ford to bring a reluctant George H. W. home from China, where he was serving as U.S. envoy, in order to take over the then (as now) discredited Central Intelligence Agency—an appointment, Rumsfeld was quoted as saying, that would "sink the sonofabitch for good."

He was wrong, but never let it be said that in all his years in Washington Donald Rumsfeld ever gave up a connivance easily. Long wars and Oval Office intrigue were always his specialty. Having marked George H. W. Bush as a rival when they served together in the U.S. House, "Rummy," as his erstwhile wrestling teammates at Princeton called him, set his jaw for a definitive takedown, no holds barred.

Nor did Rumsfeld's penchant for self-aggrandizement go unnoticed by longtime Republican insiders. In his political history *Reagan's Revolution*, Craig Shirley quotes the irrepressible Lyn Nofziger's response to a question about Rumsfeld's suitability as Reagan's vice presidential running mate in 1980: "Rummy would be fine," said

Nofziger, "but we'll have to hire a food taster for Reagan."

So there was Rummy, along with Kissinger (wearing his Metternich, rather than Strangelove, hat), working late hours to negotiate a return to personal power in a Reagan-Ford co-presidency. That their dream would never be realized seemed obvious as the negotiations dragged through the night. With three of Reagan's top aides—Ed Meese, Nofziger, and pollster Dick Wirthlin—vehemently against the deal, the overriding question remained why Ronald Reagan (not to mention Nancy) would agree to share power with a man he'd tried to remove from the White House only four years before.

But more, there was a changed political dynamic working at the 1980 Republican convention that was sure to cause trouble if Reagan for some reason had picked Gerald Ford as his vice presidential running mate.

At the party convention held in Kansas City in 1976—Ford's convention, orchestrated by his then chief of staff, Dick Cheney—the big issues on the table had to do with foreign policy and the economy. The question of how best to fight the Cold War was the litmus test that separated hard-line anti-Soviet Reagan conservatives from what they viewed as accommodationist milksops like Ford (who had refused to meet with Alexander Solzhenitsyn) and Kissinger, his secretary of state.

There would be no foreign policy debate at the 1980 convention, however. The Ford-Kissinger crowd had been routed, the old division between heartland and Eastern-seaboard Republicans swept away by the force of Ronald Reagan's charismatic hold on the party. Nor would there be any platform dispute over economic issues. The venerable Herb Stein's feet-on-the-ground approach to economic growth had given way to the exotic supply-side theory of Arthur Laffer and Robert Mundell.

The GOP of the '80s, in short, would belong to the Reaganites—not the monolithic conservative movement imagined by the mainstream media but a mixed ideological bag of Cold War hawks, free-marketers, small-government libertarians, and a militant new element at Republican conventions: the true-believing legion of religionists personified by Pat Robertson and Jerry Falwell, whose agenda involved abolishing abortion, restoring prayer in schools, and enacting a litany of socially restrictive measures designed to advance what they chose to call "family values."

Had he become Reagan's running mate, Ford, a political product of the pre–*Roe v. Wade* era, would have had an awkward time dealing with these televangelical True Believers and their messianic focus on moral issues. George H. W. Bush, the man who survived the Rumsfeld-Kissinger coup to become Reagan's running mate, would fall in with the Robertson-Falwell program, but as the campaign wore on, it became apparent, at least to those around him, that Bush didn't much care for mixing politics and religion.

Though brought up in a religious family—Bible readings by father Prescott Bush at the breakfast table each morning—everything in George H. W.'s background told him religion was a private, not a public, matter. Bush's way out of this personal dilemma was to concentrate on his strong point, foreign policy issues, and address the concerns of the Religious Right only when pressed. A decade later, as president, he would insulate himself from the issues that made up the Robertson-Falwell agenda, delegating contact with the pietist Right to his chief of staff, John Sununu, and a specially created White House office linked to what his eldest son, George W., liked to refer to as "the faith-based community."

Abortion, prayer in schools, gays in the military: The paramount issues, if not the rules of the game at Republican conventions, were changing. In the conventions that followed, it would be the social—or, more accurately, moral—issues that dominated the party's agenda in Dallas (1984), New Orleans (1988), Houston (1992), and San Diego (1996). Barry Goldwater, watching the scene from a libertarian distance, was among those traditional Republicans who didn't like what they saw. As Goldwater told Bob Dole at one point in Dole's campaign for the presidency in 1996, "I think, Bob, we're the moderates now."

Are You Washed in the Blood of the Lamb?

The Theo-Cons were not, however, as the media early on described them, "single-issue voters." From the moment they descended on the Republican convention in 1980, the Robertson-Falwell crowd had in mind a wide-spectrum

Holy Roller agenda for the party, one based on a view of the American political process as nothing less than "a moral struggle between good and evil" in which the forces of good "must be feared" and the forces of evil made to "think twice before opening their mouths."

Words lifted from a Michael Moore parody of Right-wing rhetoric? A quote from Ann Coulter on a bad hair day? Pat Robertson on a bad hemorrhoid day? None of the above. The words are those of a dead-serious manifesto for a cultural jihad led by the Free Congress Foundation, whose chairman, Paul Weyrich, has been hailed as "the godfather of the social conservative[2] movement."

And not, as Jerry Falwell could testify, without good reason. It was Weyrich in fact who gave Falwell's movement its "Moral Majority" label. The influence of Weyrich, a church deacon, as a prime mover for the Religious Right began in the early 1970s when, with the financial backing of Colorado beer baron Joseph Coors, he launched a profitable career organizing Washington think tanks and political tongs, beginning with the Heritage Foundation and Moral Majority. Their purpose? Here's the way the godfather himself put it not long after Ronald Reagan moved into the White House:

---

[2] Though "social conservative" is the term generally used to describe members of the Religious Right, Republican pollster Tony Fabrizio was the first to point out that "moral conservative" is a more precise way to define political activists like Robertson and Falwell. "Social conservatives," by Fabrizio's definition, may or may not oppose abortion rights and stem cell research, focusing instead on issues such as crime, immigration, and educational curricula and standards.

"We are different from previous generations of conservatives. We are no longer working to preserve the status quo. We are radicals, working to overturn the present power structure of this country."

It's possible that Weyrich, a relentless organizer (although he temporarily quit politics when the Senate failed to remove Clinton from office), actually believed Reagan's election sweep in 1980 would be the revolutionary beginning of the radical "overturn" he envisioned. If so, the deacon was due for a disappointment. The Great Communicator, like his political idol Franklin D. Roosevelt, could also be a Great Illusionist—all things to all voters.

Campaigning for president in 1980, Reagan had assured an ostensibly nonpartisan Moral Majority audience that, "You can't endorse me, but I can endorse you," a cheer line that encouraged social conservatives to believe that he embraced their agenda as his own. But as Lou Cannon pointed out in his 1982 biography, Reagan was "a master in using the militant fringe of his party when it served his purpose and isolating it when it did not."

Cannon cites a conversation he had with a senior Reagan aide (probably Mike Deaver) following a presidential meeting with an evangelical antiabortion group in the Oval Office. The aide, who made no secret of his opposition to the militant fringe, cautioned Cannon "not to make judgments until I saw what the Moral Majority and its allies were actually given by the administration."

"What do you want to give them?" asked Cannon, to which came a one-word reply: "Symbolism." Then, with an illuminating flourish, the Reagan aide added, "We want to keep the Moral Majority so close to us they can't move their arms."

That plan worked for the most part, but it can hardly be said the Moral Majoritarians came away with nothing but "symbolism" during the Reagan years. First, there were Theocratic funding restrictions placed on all programs, domestic and foreign, aimed at family planning, population control, or anything else that ran counter to the biblical mandate to go forth and multiply; second, there were Cabinet appointments given to such Theo-Cons as Donald Hodel who, after serving as Secretary of Energy, would become CEO of the Christian Coalition. Not to forget James Watt, Reagan's first Secretary of Interior, a fundamentalist so convinced the Apocalypse was imminent that it didn't really matter if Weyerhauser downed every tree west of Kansas City and Yellowstone was converted into a Disney theme park.

To be sure, there were in 1980—and are today—traditional church-goers against mixing religion with politics, citing Scripture to make their case (Matthew 21:21, "Render unto Caesar…"). Falwell, in fact, was once among that nonpolitical number but changed his position when the aftershock of the counter-culture revolution of the 1960s reached the outskirts of his pastoral Eden—Lynchburg, Virginia. As religious historian Steven Weldman put it, "Angry about court rulings allowing abortion and banning prayer in school, Falwell and others argued that Christians should dive aggressively into the public realm in order to promote Christian values."

Add to that the case made by religious conservatives that in moving into the public realm they're only doing what Liberal ministries like the National Council of Churches and the public preacher Jesse Jackson have been doing for decades. What's the difference, they ask, between Bill Clinton preaching Democratic salvation in African American churches and George W. preaching Republican gospel at Bob Jones University?

No difference, as far as it goes. The problem starts not when a president goes to church but when he brings the church into the White House. Bad as Clinton was in pandering for votes, he didn't turn West Wing space over to Jackson's Rainbow Coalition to hand out tens of millions of taxpayer dollars for so-called "faith-based initiatives."

But I get ahead of the invasion: All that lay two decades and five conventions away from the week in July 1980, when Pat Robertson and Jerry Falwell's True Believers launched their takeover of the party of Lincoln. Did Ronald Reagan or George H. W. Bush see the takeover coming? If they thought about it at all, it was in positive terms. For national candidates with the White House in view, votes are votes, and in the case of the True Believers, more than votes. The Christian Coalitionists and Moral Majoritarians were seen as a Republican answer to the door-to-door campaign manpower furnished the Democrats by the AFL-CIO and other labor unions.

Interested only in turnout and numbers, the party pros were exultant over the prospect of moving the church into the party and the party into the church. The evangelicals, from the sawdust trail days of William Jennings Bryan, had always been Democrats and, as with the Neo-Cons, the party pros laid out the welcome mat for crossovers. So what if the party platform read like a month of entries from Jerry Falwell's daily diary? The bottom line in politics would be Republican victories and Democratic defeats.

It would also be, from that day to the present, a cynical trade-off of political principle for numbers, standing on its head the party's traditional opposition to unwarranted government intrusion into the private lives of its citizens: Big Brother would be in the bedroom (but not, in deference to the party's financial base, the boardroom).

✶ ✶ ✶

Let me confess that along with most Republicans in Detroit that week, I hadn't seen the invasion coming, though as George H. W.'s speechwriter I'd had ample warning that Jimmy Carter's "born again" vote of four years before had crossed party lines (with ex-Carterite Pat Robertson leading the way). While the earth-shaking Republican issues in 1980 were Carter's handling of the Tehran hostage crisis and economic "malaise," time and again during the primary season we'd encounter audiences more interested in court rulings on prayer in schools, pornography, and, most seismic of all, abortion.

Seven years had passed since the Supreme Court's decision in *Roe v. Wade*, time enough to dispel any notion that abortion opponents, after a flurry of protest marches, would accept the decision as established law of the land. As predicted, the protest marches had come, but contrary to expectations, they were just the beginning of the "pro-life"[3] effort to make *Roe* a major political cause for the Republican Right.

It was history in the re-making, a Supreme Court decision accepted by most Americans but fiercely resisted and resented by a significant segment of the population: *Brown v. Topeka Board of Education* as a political precursor of *Roe v. Wade*.

As a law student at the University of Alabama in the late 1940s, I'd heard of and came to meet a progressive young state representative from Barbour County named George Wallace. Not only was Wallace a populist challenging the entrenched political establishment in Montgomery, but as a delegate to the 1948 Democratic convention in Philadelphia, he had refused to walk out with the Dixiecrat segregationists when, following a fiery speech by Minneapolis Mayor Hubert Humphrey, the party took a strong civil rights stand.

Ten years later, after *Brown v. Board of Education*, Wallace, with an opportunist's eye on the Alabama governorship, was preaching racism like a rabid Dixiecrat. After losing to a hard-line segregationist opponent in 1958, he notoriously vowed never to be "out-segged" again, and by 1963 the onetime "progressive," now governor, was acting

---

[3] An obfuscatory spin term, used with quotation marks here and throughout, along with its opposite number, "pro-choice." Whatever else might be said of antiabortion *Roe* opponents, they excel in the spin doctor's art of saccharin euphemism. Having determined that the prefix *anti-* holds a negative connotation, they successfully sold the media on the term "pro-life," leading *Roe* supporters to counter with the equally obfuscatory term "pro-choice." All of which takes me back to my own days as a professional spin doctor, circa 1962, when I represented an agri-business association that called itself the Plant Food Institute—"plant food," as in fertilizer. Big market for that, especially in Washington.

out a campaign pledge to "stand in the schoolhouse door" in order to keep black students from entering the university.

Extremism begetting extremism. To a close observer of both scenes, the parallel between the political reaction to *Brown* and the reaction to *Roe* was as appalling as it was obvious.

In Southern politics, post-*Brown*, hard-line segregationists like Wallace, Georgia Governor Lester Maddox, and South Carolina Governor Fritz Hollings left no middle ground, no room for rational debate. To run for office and be labeled "soft" on segregation was a political kiss of death. When another Alabama populist, George Hawkins, argued that the Court's decision was the law of the land, his once-promising political career was over. When a candidate for Congress launched a petition to impeach Chief Justice Earl Warren for handing down the *Brown* decision, an opposing candidate came out in favor of impeaching the *entire* U.S. Supreme Court. When a gubernatorial candidate in Georgia, Carl Sanders, was pictured shaking hands with black basketball players, his opponent, the "born-again" Jimmy Carter, saw to it that the photo was widely distributed in the rural areas of the state.

Year by year, election by election, the hard line got harder, the level of political discourse more heated, until the inflamed rhetoric of politicians trying to "out-seg" each other created an atmosphere that led to bombings, threats to the judiciary, even murder—all in the name of a Higher Calling.

Move now to the post-*Roe* decades to find the antiabortion movement raising the rhetorical stakes election by election, with Republican candidates for high office tripping over their tongues—and, where such still exist, their principles—to avoid being labeled "soft" on abortion, contraception, stem cell research, and other issues that make up the "pro-life" agenda.

In 2005, the demagoguery reached a Wallace-level nadir with the Terry Schiavo case. Layering tragedy with farce, a purportedly conservative Republican majority in Congress made a national cause célèbre out of a Florida case involving a husband's right to terminate life support to his brain-dead wife, against the wishes of the wife's mother and father. When the Florida courts, in a succession of rulings, held that he did have the right, a consortium of Holy Rollers (and their talk show flacks) zeroed in on the Schiavo case and in short order had their political minions from Capitol Hill to the White House jumping through pharisaical hoops on behalf of "the culture of life."

Terri Schiavo would go to her rest in March 2005, after having been shamefully exploited by the likes of Senate Majority Leader Bill Frist, House Majority Leader Tom DeLay, and a host of professional Bible-wingers. Frist, a heart surgeon, went so far as to quack up an optimistic diagnosis of the patient based on a video clip, while DeLay was pistol-whipping the House into passing legislation to transfer jurisdiction from state to federal court, a bill the president—with an alacrity missing when Hurricane Katrina struck—rushed back to Washington to sign.

It was one of those sordid post-Goldwater moments in 21st-century political history when, like Pete Hamill, I could only wish the old maverick were still around to call a travesty a goddamn travesty.

Goldwater was an all-but-forgotten figure at the Republican convention of 1980, the mantle of conservative leadership having passed to the new hero of the political right, Ronald Reagan. Nor did the old maverick play a significant role as a policy advisor in the half-decade he served in the Senate during the Reagan presidency. But in one key presidential decision—Reagan's appointment of the first woman justice on the U.S. Supreme Court—it was Barry Goldwater's recommendation of Sandra Day O'Connor that carried the day. It also earned the strident opposition of the Moral Majority's Jerry Falwell.

Falwell's objection to the O'Connor appointment was based on her having co-sponsored a bill in the Arizona legislature providing for "medically accepted family-planning methods and information" to those who asked for it. To the head of the Moral Majority and other True Believers, the nomination of anyone backing a bill of that sort ran counter to the 1980 Republican platform pledge to appoint only judges "who respect traditional family values and the sanctity of human life."

For Goldwater, this attack on a friend and fellow Arizonan was the tipping point in his relations with what he called "the checkbook clergy." In his 1988 autobiography, the Arizona senator, recalling the televangelical assault on O'Connor, went even further in his criticism of officious "clergy engaged in a heavy-handed, continuing attempt to use political means to obtain moral ends—and vice-versa...

"It is one of the most dangerous trends in the country," wrote Goldwater. "They are attempting to institutionalize politics in their churches...We don't have to look back centuries to see the danger in that. Look at the carnage in the name of religious righteousness in Iran. The long and bloody division of Northern Ireland. The Christian-Moslem and Moslem-Moslem 'holy war' in Lebanon."

Written in the final year of the Reagan presidency, Goldwater's cautionary words were predictably ignored by the holy warriors, then wrapping up the first stage of their capture of the Republican party. The second stage would come with the Republican takeover of Congress—but not before the "symbolism" of the Reagan era was followed by the appointment of an evangelical activist to an influential position inside the George H. W. Bush White House in 1989.

His name was Doug Wead and he was personally selected for the White House post by the president's newly reborn son, George W., who perceived a need for someone to act as his father's ambassador/liaison to "the faith-based community." It was a pietist prelude to George W.'s establishing the first White House Office of Religion and Morality a dozen years later. (No, they don't call it that; under Karl Rove's Orwellian dictum it's been euphemized into "the White House Office of Faith-Based and Community Initiatives.")

Wead's ambassadorship to the Religious Right wasn't enough to save George H. W. from losing the 1992 election, but for Wead himself the experience was a case of onward and spiritually, if not politically, upward: On leaving his White House post he traveled west to run as the Republican candidate for an open congressional seat in Arizona. Better he'd pulled up in Albuquerque.

Though Wead was from Arizona, his running for office in what was then Goldwater country proved politically disastrous. Not only did Barry, still furious at the "checkbook clergy," jump party lines to vote for Wead's Democratic opponent—who won, going away—but the old maverick, at his bristling best, also denounced George W.'s evangelical soul mate as a cross between "an Amway salesman and Jerry Falwell."

Not bad as political descriptives go. In fact, a fairly apt limning of the sort of candidate young Dubya himself aspired to be as he looked down the road toward his own political future.

Chapter 3

NEWT AND THE DESTROYERS: ENTER THE 104TH CONGRESS

Gingrich May Run in 2008 If No Front-Runner Emerges
—HEADLINE, *WASHINGTON POST*, JUNE 10, 2006

P ARTIES IN TODAY'S MEDIA-CENTRIC political world are defined as much by the televised face they show the public as by their platforms and position papers. For the party occupying the White House, the face is that of the president, but for the party out of power—as Democrats have painfully learned in recent years—there's a blurred image problem: No power center, no clear focus on what the party stands for.

Republicans had no such problem on taking control of Congress in January 1995, however. The Democrats still owned the White House, but a clear and omnipresent face, that of Speaker Newton Leroy Gingrich, would not only define but also set the course for the GOP as it moved into the 21st century under his leadership.

It all started with Newt's "Contract with America," a ten-point program drawn up by Gingrich and his House leadership team (Dick Armey, Tom DeLay, John Kasich, Bill Paxon, Bob Walker) to advance Republican prospects in the 1994 congressional campaign. The Contract, said Newt, represented a solemn pledge not only to reform House procedure after forty years of Democratic maladministration but also to "transform" the country's political landscape by rolling back the Liberal tide of laws and regulations initiated by Democratic administrations from Franklin Roosevelt's New Deal to Lyndon Johnson's Great Society.

How significant was the "revolutionary" Contract? Viewed in retrospect a dozen years later, it seems no more than a blip on the political radar screen. But at the time, Gingrich, a former professor from West Georgia college, was content to tell reporters, "There is no comparable congressional document in our two-hundred-year history."

That said, the incomparable document was aimed, according to its ambitious framers, at controlling the growth of government with a balanced budget; reforming both the welfare and legal systems; "unleashing" the economy by freeing American business from excessive government regulation; providing "middle class tax relief" (along with tax cuts for the "unleashed" upper class); bolstering national defense; and enacting term limit legislation "to replace career politicians with citizen legislators."

The Contract contained ten clauses, all to be passed by the House in one hundred days. The most important clause, as Gingrich saw it, was the pledge to balance the budget by the year 2002. That would be the first priority of the first session of the 104th Congress.

Newt never doubted his ability to push through a Republican budget bill over the opposition of Bill Clinton's White House. The GOP now had the votes in both houses of Congress, which made the Clinton presidency, as Gingrich policy guru Grover Norquist put it, "irrelevant."

Underestimating the Liberal in the White House would be only the first of a series of miscalculations leading to Gingrich's fall from power four years later.

✳ ✳ ✳

To Tip O'Neill, all politics was local; to Newt Gingrich, it was all personal. When in 1987 Newt leveled his sights on then House Speaker Jim Wright for pocketing a six-figure advance on a sweetheart book deal, it wasn't enough to make his case on ethical grounds and let the facts speak for themselves; he attacked the Democratic Speaker in personal terms and obviously relished doing it. As Gingrich told Tom Fiedler of the *Miami Herald*, Wright wasn't simply "the most corrupt Speaker in the 20th century," he was also "so consumed by his own power that he is like Mussolini." There was, added Gingrich, "overwhelming evidence" of Jim Wright's "grotesque" corruption and his being not only "a bald-faced liar" but also "a genuinely bad man."

It was Newt at his most rabid, the sort of unmuzzled-Doberman attack that endeared him to militant Right activists frustrated by what they regarded as the mealy-mouthed temperance of Republican spokesmen like House Minority Leader Bob Michels as well as Senate Leader Bob Dole, dismissed by Gingrich as a Kansas-bred "tax collector for the welfare state."

The irony contained in that classic Gingrichism was that Newt himself had scrim-thin conservative credentials. His reputation as a hard-line Right-winger was based more on the Liberal enemies he made than on any set of conservative principles he espoused. Russell Kirk and Richard Weaver weren't on his recommended reading list to freshman Republican congressmen, though Third Wave futurists like Alvin and Heidi Toffler were. He would lead the Republican chorus against taxes and Big Government as long as the Democrats were in control, but once the reins of power passed into Republican hands, he became more interested in, as he framed it, "using the resources of the federal government" to reshape society along the expansive Tofflerian lines he favored.

Though Gingrich's prime focus was on domestic affairs, the new Speaker had no problem expressing his opinion, solicited or not, on foreign policy issues as well. There, too, his positions were often contrary to those of conservative Republicans, breaking ranks, for example, to support U.S. intervention in Kosovo at a time when even Texas Governor George W. Bush stood opposed to U.S. engagement in "nation building."

It was a hint of things to come a decade later when, with Republicans in control of both the executive and legislative branches, Gingrich, as a member of Donald Rumsfeld's inner circle of advisors, would emerge in full Neo-Con plumage; altogether fitting for a bipolar political personality who, while sworn to destroy all things Democratic, would tell reporter Elizabeth Drew that his favorite American president was "FDR, the greatest leader we ever had."

The contradictions in Newt Gingrich's political life didn't stop there. Though as Speaker he would rouse Republican audiences with outraged denunciations of his *least* favorite American president, Bill Clinton, Newt had more in common with the Liberal in the White House than he'd care to admit (or would want his adulatory partisan fans to hear about).

Forget the serial womanizing both engaged in; that would come later. Like Clinton, Gingrich grew up as a mama's boy and took the surname of a rough-hewn stepfather he didn't like; spent his formative years as a social outsider in a small Southern town; avoided military service as a student during the Vietnam War; took part in the counter-cultural student rebellion of the 1960s (including an "experiment" with marijuana); and had his wonkish butt kicked in his first run for political office, a losing race for Congress.

From a conservative viewpoint, however, the most striking similarity between the Liberal in the White House in 1995 and the newly installed Speaker of the House was their ability to revise personal experience to meet their political needs: Clinton, for example, could remember the burning of black churches in Arkansas in the 1950s that no other Arkansan, black or white, could recall, while Gingrich could conveniently alter the scenario of his first Republican convention when a *Los Angeles Times* reporter later asked how he came to support Liberal favorite Nelson Rockefeller in the 1968 race for the Republican presidential nomination.

"Because," replied the Speaker, in all sincerity, "my real candidate, Ronald Reagan, wasn't in the race." Such recall of events came as a surprise to hundreds of GOP convention delegates at Miami Beach that year who not only voted for then-governor Reagan for president but also came within a hairsbreadth of denying Richard Nixon the nomination.

A Jim Wright-like "bald-faced lie" on Newt's part? Let's be generous: It's simply the West Georgia history professor as an alternative-history professor.

✶ ✶ ✶

Though Beltway table talk and his own political spin team gave Newt and his Contract full credit for having produced the Republican sweep of '94, the polls argued otherwise. Surveys showed that outside Washington few people had even heard of the Contract and of these, only 4 percent said it had any influence on the way they voted. What did account for voters turning against congressional Democrats in 1994, however, was a series of House scandals reflecting an arrogance of power brought on by four decades of one-party rule.

Since the sweep hadn't been confined to Republican victories in House races—the GOP won not only the U.S. Senate but also state houses from Albany to Austin—

another factor, beyond Democratic problems on the Hill, was obviously at work. Pollsters found it at the other end of Pennsylvania Avenue, in the Clinton White House: Hillary Clinton's 1993 push for a comprehensive health care program had not only foundered in Congress but brought her husband's approval ratings down by double-digit numbers.

"We ran against Clinton that year," recalls one member of the Class of '94, since retired from Congress. "Newt running around, bragging to the press about how he'd nationalized the election when it was really Bubba in the White House who did it. The Democrats didn't even want him in their districts. He was absolute poison."

This was a fair appraisal of the forty-second president's political status in January 1995. His party repudiated on Capitol Hill, Bill Clinton stood alone, an apparent lame duck, the butt of late-night television jokes—a sure sign, as a TV critic once wrote, of a politician's decline and fall.

Then suddenly, fortuitously for James Carville, George Stephanopoulos, and other members of the Clinton spin squad, their low-polling, overexposed client no longer occupied center stage: The Clinton luck—second only to resilience as his strongest political suit—had blessed him with a flamboyant antagonist addicted to the spotlight.

* * *

For Bill Clinton, as with most politicians, getting attention was a means of acquiring power; for Newt Gingrich, the acquisition of power had always been the means of getting what he could never get enough of—attention. In the days and weeks following his investiture as Speaker—through January, February, and into early spring—no twenty-four-hour period passed in Washington without one or more Gingrich press briefings, and no weekend was complete without the *Time* magazine cover boy ("The Gingrich Who Stole Christmas") making Monday morning head-lines on one or more national talk shows.

Newt became, in the words of one Republican cam-paign consultant, "the Great Over-Communicator." Capitol Hill rumors had it that he had his eye set on the other end of Pennsylvania avenue, the White House itself, though his Senate friend Trent Lott was heard to ask, "What would he want to do that for? We already have a dysfunctional President."

But not all the attention the new Speaker received was the kind he and his co-revolutionaries in the House wanted. At the heart of their revolution had been the promise of a Morning in America that would bring high ethical standards to a people's House degraded by the old Democratic regime, Jim Wright's book deal the example frequently cited. Yet within days after the mid-term elec-tion, Newt had agreed to pocket a $4.5 million advance on a book contract with HarperCollins, the Rupert Murdoch–owned publishing house.

Like all self-righteous "reformers" convinced they have a cabalist relationship with the Almighty, the new Speaker saw nothing hypocritical about a lucrative book deal with his good friend Rupert. But after pressure from the media and his own troubled colleagues, Gingrich finally agreed, however reluctantly, to give up the advance and tough it out on post-publication royalties. Still, the controversy served as an amber-light portent in two areas critical to the future of the Republican party:

- First, it served notice that the new House leadership, far from reforming the corrupt practices of the old Democratic regime, meant to expand and refine them. The K-Street lobbyists would flourish, the only difference being they'd line up in front of House Whip Tom DeLay's, rather than Dan Rostenkowski's, office.

  "We found out in a hurry why they called DeLay 'the Hammer'," recalls one corporate executive, since retired. "The Democrats were out, the Republicans were in, and we not only had to kick in with campaign contributions to his PAC, but if we knew what was good for us, hire Republican lobbyists."

- The second warning signal sent by the aborted Gingrich-Murdoch book deal was that, contrary to the promise made (in a *Washington Post* interview) to abandon his reckless, Manichean ways of the past, Newt was the same old Newt, made more so by his newfound power. In the months that followed, the new Speaker would, after a series of gaffes, verbal missteps, and blunders born of hubris, become the most divisive political figure in America (replacing the "irrelevant" President who, with the counsel of chameleon advisor Dick Morris, was plotting his comeback).

It wasn't the first time Newt had promised to reform, but, like an alcoholic falling off the wagon, he quickly reverted to his old indulgent habits. National capital reporters could always count on the Gentleman from West Georgia for a red-meat quote on a slow news day, e.g.:

- When news reports told of a grisly killing in Chicago—a pregnant woman murdered and her body eviscerated—the Speaker launched into an anti-Liberal tirade, offering the case as an example of "what the welfare state has created."

- Asked what new ideas he had on furnishing government aid to dependent children, the Speaker touted a return to the old orphanage system, citing it as a way to reduce costs.

- On one occasion, testifying before a congressional committee, the hyperventilating Speaker dismissed the idea of campaign finance reform as "nonsensical socialist analysis based on hatred of the free-enterprise system."

Predictably, these off-the-wall Gingrichisms took their toll on the Speaker's—and the Republican majority's—public image. But worse was yet to come when Newt, meeting with a reporters' breakfast group in November 1995, went into the how-and-why of the government shutdown brought on by an impasse in budget talks between the Clinton White House and the Republican Congress.

Though balancing the budget was an enduring conservative goal, Newt's hard-line approach to bringing it about bordered, in the view of some Republican strategists, on the reckless. The seven-year plan put forward by the Speaker would cut $270 billion out of the Medicare program, a move guaranteed to alienate some 33 million senior citizens, the overwhelming number of whom were duly registered voters.

Republican National Committee Chairman Haley Barbour openly questioned the Speaker's push for a massive funding cut in a politically volatile area where Democrats were poised to charge the party's candidates with heartlessness toward the elderly. Dating back to the New Deal era, the charge had consistently put Republican candidates on the defensive, costing the party critical votes in close elections. Gingrich, however, was adamant, rejecting all suggestions that the Medicare cutback be deferred until after the 1996 presidential election.

The question asked by Barbour and other long-view Republican strategists was, *Why?* Why engage Clinton on Medicare, an issue that works in his favor, when by riding a conservative wave we can deal with the budget in two years with Bob Dole or some other Republican in the White House?

The politically charitable answer to that question was that after forty years of watching tax-and-spend Democrats set the fiscal agenda, conservative Republicans were impatient to put their own ideas into action. A less charitable (and, in hindsight, more sustainable) view is that Gingrich and his faux-revolutionary cohorts arrogantly assumed that Bill Clinton had the fight knocked out of him by the mid-term election results and, when faced with a strong-willed Republican Congress, would fold under pressure.

It was a misreading of both the Liberal in the White House and the mood of the country. There would be major spending cuts in other areas, but Clinton's use of the veto held the line in the battle over Medicare—a battle which, as Haley Barbour had foreseen, would cost the Republican party dearly in the presidential election of 1996.

✳ ✳ ✳

Speaker Gingrich's attendance at the mid-November meeting of the venerable Godfrey Sperling press breakfast came two days after the government shutdown. Months of negotiations had ended in a stalemate, with Clinton, politically revitalized by his defense of Medicare, consistently outmaneuvering his Republican opponents.

It had been a risky game of political chicken, each side thinking the other would be blamed for cutting off federal funds to government agencies, including the park service. In the event, as White House polls had predicted, the Republican Congress took the fall, its approval rating plunging to new lows. Even the GOP's business base, usually heard railing about federal agency interference in the free market, was unhappy with the party's congressional leadership: "Closing down the government isn't conservatism," one Washington business executive told me the day the shutdown began. "It's *radicalism!*"

Newt would have disagreed, of course, arguing that defending Congress's power of the purse was consummate conservatism. Besides, he would tell reporters at the Sperling breakfast, it was Clinton who'd triggered the shutdown by his high-handed treatment of the Speaker of the House during their recent trip aboard Air Force One for the funeral of Yitzhak Rabin: "This is petty," conceded Gingrich on being asked why he'd pushed for the shutdown. "But you land at Andrews Air Force Base and you've been on the plane for twenty-five hours and nobody has talked to you, and they ask you to get off the plane *by the back ramp*! Where is their sense of manners? Where is their sense of decency?"

So that was it. The federal government had been closed down, the people's business put on hold, for no reason other than Newt Gingrich's pique on being asked to deplane from the rear rather than the front of Air Force One. It was a signature moment in Newt Gingrich's tenure as House Speaker, a gaffe immediately seized upon by the White House to portray the president's Republican opponents in Congress as petulant extremists, though Newt's ebullient sidekick, Budget Committee Chairman John Kasich, would later look back on the shutdown as "one of the greatest moments of my career."

Easy for Kasich to say. But it would be Bob Dole, the Republican presidential nominee in 1996, who'd pay the price for the Ohio number-cruncher's "greatest moment," while Kasich and Newt bailed out of their "revolution" a few years later to make millions in the private sector.

* * *

Barry Goldwater had seen a parallel between the Republican 80th Congress that helped Harry Truman win the presidential election of 1948 and the Republican 104th Congress that would give Bill Clinton the traction he needed to win reelection in 1996. Whatever their similarities, however, there was one major difference between the 80th and the 104th:

Over half of the newly arrived Republican members of the House in January 1995 owed their election to the support of Pat Robertson's Christian Coalition and its manipulative executive director Ralph Reed. Together with senior Republicans linked to Robertson and Reed—a group that included Majority Leader Dick Armey, Whip Tom DeLay, and Budget Chairman John Kasich—the zealous newcomers would wield sufficient power to change both the character and the direction of the party traditional conservatives regarded as home.

Religiosity is nothing new in American politics, its roots going back to George Washington's addition of the words "So help me God" to his oath of office. On the benign side, church and Bible have been routinely used as a rhetorical tool in presidential campaigns, prime examples being William Jennings Bryan's "Cross of Gold" speech, Teddy Roosevelt exhorting his fellow Bull Moosers to "stand at Armageddon and battle for the Lord" in 1912, and Dwight Eisenhower's call for an ecumenical "crusade" to cleanse the political stables in 1952.

On a darker side, however, from the Know-Nothing era of the early 1800s to the election of John F. Kennedy in 1960, we've seen anti-Catholic bias fueled by radical fundamentalism as an ongoing strain in national politics. Even today, half a century after Kennedy's presidency, the same animus, now directed at Mormons, could stand in the way of Massachusetts Governor Mitt Romney's bid for the Republican presidential nomination in 2008.

Whatever their influence at the polls, however, True Believers have been less than successful in making their Theocratic agenda the law of the land. There was the Noble Experiment of the 1920s, of course, foisted on America's Immoral Majority by the precursors of the Pat and Jerry crowd. But the political backlash to the Prohibition era was such as to validate the view held by the agnostic Ambrose Bierce that more immigrants came to America seeking freedom *from* religion than did seeking freedom *of* religion.

With that in mind, Gingrich's pollster Frank Luntz argued against efforts by the Bible-thumping Republican whip, Tom DeLay, to include the Christian Coalition wish list of "moral" issues in the Contract with America. The idea behind the Contract, Luntz pointed out, was to energize conservative voters by focusing on issues that unified the base—tax cuts, welfare reform, reduced federal spending—not issues that fueled the fires of what Paul Weyrich had labeled "the culture war."

But though frustrated in their effort to get abortion, school prayer, and a ban on gays in the military included in the Contract, the true-believing wing of the House Republican conference had no problem slipping items from their Theo-Con agenda into virtually every area of legislative business that came before the 104th Congress.

Federal funds for condoms in the worldwide campaign against AIDS? That would only encourage sexual promiscuity (and who are we to say that AIDS isn't God's judgment on those who transgress against natural law?). Taxpayer money for family planning? Not when Theo-Con congressmen like New Jersey's Chris Smith and Oklahoma's Tom Coburn believed that "family planning" is simply a Liberal euphemism for abortion; not to mention an egregious misuse of the word "family."

Family Values

According to *Safire's New Political Dictionary*, the concept first appeared as a Theo-Con "attack term" in the presidential campaign of 1992, with Pat Robertson assailing Bill and Hillary Clinton for trying to "destroy the traditional family." As Safire extrapolates, "Implicit in the phrase's celebration is that the opposite side takes a permissive attitude regarding abortion and homosexual rights, undermining the institution of the family."

By the mid-'90s, the "attack term" had become so much a part of the Theo-Con campaign arsenal it was used interchangeably with "American values," a marriage of theology and patriotism embraced by Smith, Coburn, and other members of the Republican Family Caucus who would gather in prayer, heads bowed, hands joined, to rejoice each day in doing God's work. But never so much as in the fall and winter of 1998, when the psalm-singing prosecutor Kenneth Starr laid out his case for impeaching Bill Clinton.

✳ ✳ ✳

All things considered, it was fitting that Gingrich's four turbulent years as Speaker of the House should end with an exercise in political masturbation. Don't bother to look that one up in *Safire's New Political Dictionary*. It's my way of describing any political act or course of action that serves no purpose other than to make the actor feel good— even if the act is politically counter-productive.

When congressional Democrats chose to focus public attention on the Contra half of the Reagan administration's Iran-Contra scandal in 1986, they were not only engaging in a political jerk-off, but also doing the Reagan-Bush team a huge favor, one measurable in electoral votes.

Consider: How much difference would it have made in the presidential campaign of 1988 if George H. W. Bush had been called on to answer the question, "Why did your administration sell arms to the Ayatollah?" instead of "Why did your administration furnish aid to the Contras?" A major difference, in my opinion. Whether enough to have changed the election's outcome, I can't say. What I do know, having worked for George Bush in that campaign, is that defending the sale of missile launchers to the Ayatollah would have been a hell of a lot harder than defending aid to the contras in Nicaragua.

That being the case, why then didn't the Democrats emphasize the Iran side of the scandal in making their case against Bush? Other than sheer stupidity (always a possibility in Democratic presidential campaigns), there's no answer to that other than ideological force of habit: Venting outrage at Republican administrations for backing anti-Communist coups in Latin America—from Guatemala in the 1950s to Chile in the 1970s—is for Democrats a matter of self-gratification. It just felt good.

So it was, little more than a decade later, that the frustrated Theo-Cons of the Gingrich "revolution," having been outmaneuvered by Bill Clinton in 1995, then trounced in the presidential election of 1996, concluded that their only God-given recourse was to impeach the draft-dodging, skirt-chasing, duplicitous son-of-a-bitch— no matter what the opinion polls said.

On that last point, the numbers were again clear: Though Clinton's popular vote never rose above the mid-forties in either 1992 or 1996 and his polling negatives remained high through two presidential terms, the vast majority of Americans—eight out of ten in some polls— opposed his removal from office on grounds of sexual misconduct. Which isn't to say they thought well of their president having an illicit affair with a thong-snapping female intern in the Oval Office; only that, with the economy thriving and no foreign crises cluttering the evening news, they thought Congress had better things to do than delve into Bill Clinton's wenching behavior.

So why did House Republicans, given to reading polls with their morning juice, choose to hold impeachment hearings in the face of public disapproval? To True Believers like Tom DeLay, the reason lay in Bill Clinton's being "the representative of the demoralization of my generation." As Lou Dubose and Jan Reid put it in *The Hammer Comes Down*, mere mention of Clinton "made DeLay twitch with agitation."

In Kenneth W. Starr, the son of a Pentecostal Texas preacher, DeLay found a fellow obsessive. Republicans in previous years had been outraged by the partisan excess of Independent Counsel Lawrence Walsh in his squid-like investigation of Iran-Contra (ending with indictments suspiciously handed down the weekend before the 1992 presidential election). Now, at first chance, they hypocritically backed an open-ended inquisition of the Clinton White House conducted by a prosecutor willing and eager to stretch, bend, and mutilate the law to accommodate his self-defined moral imperative.

The impeachment of Bill Clinton and the Starr Report have been dealt with at length in scores of books, articles, and monographs over the past decade. Suffice it to say here that Kenneth Starr's disregard of constitutional niceties in running the Office of the Independent Counsel (e.g., the goon-like use of federal agents to intimidate witnesses and coerce testimony) presaged things to come when John Ashcroft, the lawyer son of another Pentecostal preacher, took over the Department of Justice in 2001.

And what was the Speaker of the House doing while all this was going on? So outraged was Newt Gingrich at Bill Clinton's scandalous behavior that he vowed to let no day pass without rising to condemn it—this while Gingrich himself, as his wife later discovered, was carrying on a five-year affair with a House aide a quarter-century his junior.

Newt for president in 2008? Déjà vu all over again. But the fact that he's taken seriously tells us all we need to know about the change that's taken place in the Republican party since the days of Barry Goldwater.

Chapter 4

LIKE FATHER,
UNLIKE SON

"Dad's naïve."

—GEORGE W. BUSH, QUOTED RE HIS FATHER'S DEALINGS

WITH CONGRESSIONAL LEADERS, CIRCA FALL, 1991

O N HIS FINAL DAY in office, George H. W. Bush, like all departing presidents, was afforded one last trip aboard Air Force One. It is a lonely flight for most ex-presidents, but Bush, a compulsive optimist, thought to brighten the day by inviting friends and former staffers to join him on his return to Houston.

The three-hour flight was a time for reminiscence and second thoughts—none, however, having to do with the recent election, a subject still raw in Bush's memory. But when the subject turned to his relations with Democratic congressional leaders, the former president, though not bitter, had serious second thoughts about his dealings with Senate Majority Leader George Mitchell and House Speaker Tom Foley.

"They kept saying, 'We're here to help get your program through,'" Bush recalled. "It took me a long time to realize they didn't mean to help at all." Naïve George—at least in his eldest son's eyes.

Entering the Oval Office as President in January 2001, young George was determined not to repeat his father's mistakes. Some things are in the hands of God and out of a president's control, but in matters where he had the last word—where he was the Decider—there would be no naïveté in the way this President Bush dealt with Democrats *or* the national media *or* members of his own staff. The old man had put his trust in too many people with self-serving agendas; the new White House staff, with the exception of Andy Card and his deputy Joe Hagin, would be a tight circle of Texans, people he knew prized loyalty above all else.

Card, the new White House chief of staff and a Bush loyalist for over twenty years, was the lone eye witness that wintry afternoon when the two presidents, Bush (43) and Bush (41), went into the Oval Office, Dubya moving behind the massive executive desk for the first time, then looking across the room at his father. Not a word was said, recalls Card: "They just looked at each other and smiled."[1]

---

[1] A more melodramatic version of the scene, set out by Todd Purdum in the September 2006 issue of *Vanity Fair*, has both Georges breaking into sobs. Not so. The only known politician in tears on that particular inaugural day was Al Gore.

By no means, however, was the scene Card described on the order of what had taken place forty years before, when Joe Kennedy watched his son enter the Oval Office for the first time. The Kennedy patriarch was a kingmaker who saw Jack as only the first in a line of Kennedy presidents; in contrast, the Bush patriarch was inclined by neither background nor temperament to think in terms of political dynasty.

"Politics was hardly ever the subject of dinner-table conversation around the house," according to Marvin Bush, the youngest of George and Barbara's four sons. "We had other things to talk about."

Indeed they did. Politics to the Bushes was a matter of civic obligation, not a family obsession. Working in the 1980 campaign I soon concluded, as did most members of the staff, that other than Barbara, the only member of the family who had any real impact on voters was Jeb, a crowd-pleasing orator in two languages. After watching him work up a Spanish-speaking audience one sweltering Miami afternoon, I told a fellow staffer that whether his father won or lost that campaign, Jeb was one Bush with a political future.

It wasn't that Dubya lacked political skills. He had his father's grasp of campaign organization, along with the old man's gift of memory for names and faces. While less than impressive as a public speaker, in a one-on-one exchange and before small groups he displayed a down-home personality that broke through social barriers—the Texas straight-shooter image he honed to perfection, as both governor and president.

Dubya did, however, have his drawbacks as a campaign surrogate. He had an unfortunate penchant for making publicity waves by talking too freely (and flippantly) to members of the traveling press: off-the-wall statements that made for unwanted items in the "Periscope" section of *Newsweek*. But there was never a hint in any of his father's campaigns that young George had a problem with alcohol or a strained relationship with the old man.

That story line would surface later, in the mid-'80s, along with talk about how George H. W., then vice president, had called on his friend Billy Graham to pay a summer visit to the Bush home in Kennebunkport, Maine, where, in walks along the beach, God's American Vicar, as young George relates in his autobiography, "planted a mustard seed in my soul."

$$* \quad * \quad *$$

"There's a higher father I appeal to."
—GEORGE W. BUSH, ON BEING ASKED BY BOB WOODWARD WHETHER HE CONSULTED GEORGE H. W. BEFORE MAKING THE DECISION TO INVADE IRAQ

On reading that huffy holy-roller response to a mundane question, my first thought was that young George was up to his old tricks, throwing out a flippant line to see how his listener reacted. Then I thought again: This wasn't the cocky, unburdened candidate's son we'd known in the '80s who'd "had a good week" because he'd struck a well and his old man had been nominated vice president. This was the President of the United States, sitting in the

Oval Office, with reminders all around that words have consequences.

Not that the old flippancy hadn't occasionally slipped through the cracks, even after Dubya took office—the macho frat boy doing his imitation of Sylvester Stallone ("Bring it on!") or calling for the capture of Osama bin Laden, Texas Ranger-style, "dead or alive." But in this case I read into his answer something more calculated—a gratuitous put-down of the man who'd done more than any other (Karl Rove's claim to the contrary) to put him in the White House.

Whatever the motive behind young George's disdainful response, however, it sent a signal that he intended to put distance between his presidency and that of his father. Washington insiders had surmised as much from the way top and mid-level political positions were being filled in the Bush-II administration. With a few notable exceptions—Dick Cheney, Colin Powell, Condoleezza Rice, Andy Card, Josh Bolten—everyone connected with the Bush-I presidency had been frozen out of anything having to do with policy. More than that, the selection of George H. W. Bush's most bitter political enemy, Donald Rumsfeld, as Secretary of Defense signaled not only distance but also a wall between the two Bush presidencies.

Why Rumsfeld? Powell's appointment as Secretary of State made sense because of his prestige and popularity. Rice was a good fit to head the National Security Council because of her experience and supposed expertise. But why bring back a political relic from the Cold War era when there were half-a-dozen candidates for the job who were younger and better attuned to the nation's defense needs in a post–Cold War world?

It wasn't as if Rumsfeld brought anything to the table politically. As Secretary of Defense in the Ford administration, the arrogant Illinois martinet had made more enemies than friends. But as happens in Washington (with notable frequency in the Bush-II years), the appointee had a crony in the right place—a friend with clout enough to pluck him out of political obscurity and thrust him into the unlikely role of defense secretary for the son of a man whose political career he'd more than once tried to bury.

It was naïve George, all right, but the son, not the father: By reuniting the megalomaniacal team of Dick Cheney and Donald Rumsfeld, the young inexperienced president had put a finishing touch on his vice president's Byzantine plan to run the executive branch of the United States government by proxy.

"When Cheney talks, it's Bush."

—*Weekly Standard* editor William Kristol

In 1996, Dick Cheney, having surveyed the political landscape and decided that running for president required more time and effort than he was willing to give, hit on a more practical mid-life career strategy: He would forget politics, though not the political friends who could help him accumulate as much money as was humanly possible in the remaining years of his life.

Four years later, debating with Joe Lieberman, his Democratic counterpart running for vice president, Dick would answer Lieberman's reference to how rich he'd become as Halliburton's chief executive by acknowledging yes, he'd made a lot of money, but "Government had nothing to do with it."

Lieberman, having learned the art of political debate from his running mate, Al Gore, then proceeded to blow an opportunity to knock one out of the park by merely grinning his most ingratiating Alfred E. Neuman grin and waving to his mother in the audience.

Government has nothing to do with Halliburton's profits? If it didn't, Dick Cheney would never have been hired as its CEO.

The unsettling thought is that in the hall of mirrors Dick Cheney wakes up in every morning, he may very well believe that Halliburton's bottom line is immaculately conceived. A man who in the third year of the Iraq war could insist that, by God, there *are* weapons of mass destruction, or *were*, until Saddam slipped them across the Syrian border into the hands of Osama bin Laden, is likely to believe anything (and insist that you believe it as well).

To be sure, this wasn't the Dick Cheney Americans bargained for when he became George W. Bush's running mate in the summer of 2000—the modulated public figure we saw in charge of the Pentagon, sharing the stage with Colin Powell during the first Gulf war. Or maybe it was the same Cheney, but we didn't see his dark side because he was clever enough to mask it while in the service of a president who wouldn't tolerate a manipulative Secretary of Defense with his own war agenda.

It was no secret back then that in the last hours of the first Gulf War, Cheney had urged George H. W. to finish Saddam Hussein off—marching to Baghdad, if necessary—while Colin Powell urged restraint, arguing that if Bush followed that course it would lead into a Vietnam-like morass. "We've finished what we set out to do," said Powell. "We've run Saddam out of Kuwait and crippled his army: Let's call it the One Hundred Hour War, declare victory, and bring the troops home."

The fact that Powell won that argument did not, to understate the case, sit well with his boss, the Secretary of Defense. "Generals," said Cheney acidly, "should stick to military matters and leave politics and diplomacy to their civilian superiors." None of this resentment was apparent to President Bush, however, because Cheney knew Bush had no patience for backbiting or second-guessing among members of his inner circle.

On the contrary, the Defense secretary, when later asked about the decision to stop short of regime change in Baghdad, dutifully followed the party line laid down by Powell and NSC director Brent Scowcroft: "We couldn't push on," Cheney told those who questioned the decision to stop short of Baghdad. "The alliance the President put together would have collapsed and we'd have had to go it alone."

Little did those of us who heard that answer realize that beneath Dick Cheney's stoic façade lay the heart and mind of a triumphalist Neo-Con who didn't give a damn whether we had allies joining us or not: *We're a Superpower,* was (and remains) Cheney's mindset. *Let's act like one. Bombs away!*

At Halliburton headquarters in Texas in the late 1990s Cheney let it be known to those in Washington, who asked his expert opinion, that all the Clinton White House chatter about a "peace bonus" emerging from the end of the Cold War was so much Liberal pacifist bullshit. "We still have enemies out there," he argued. "This isn't the right time to cut back on the defense budget." (Not that there would ever be a right time for Halliburton stockholders.)

First and foremost among the enemies that Halliburton's CEO had in mind, of course, was his old nemesis Saddam, flourishing in Baghdad because Bob Woodward's friend Colin Powell (Cheney had only contempt for the way Powell played up to the press) had won that pivotal argument in the Oval Office back in 1991. When, in 1998, the Project for a New American Century, the heavy-breathing Neo-Con agitprop group launched by Richard Perle and William Kristol, wrote an open letter to the Clinton White House calling for "removing Saddam Hussein from power," Cheney, though not a signatory because of his position at Halliburton, was there in spirit through his friend Don Rumsfeld, whose name was high on the list of signers.

Meanwhile, in another part of Texas, Governor George W. Bush was coasting through his race for reelection as governor, looking two years ahead to the presidential campaign of 2000 and, with the help of his father, putting together a cadre of experts that would give him a crash course in foreign and domestic policy: Colin Powell, Condoleezza Rice, Brent Scowcroft, Andy Card, and other experienced hands from the first Bush administration.

They would all find their way to Dubya's sagebrush Xanadu in Crawford, Texas, for weekend sessions aimed at preparing their host for the press inquisition sure to come in a presidential campaign.

Along with Dick Cheney, of course. By all means, George the Elder would recommend Dick to serve as dean of his son's Crawford Institute of Policy Studies. Dick would be the old man's surrogate, a mature, responsible voice steering the boy clear of anything rash, in word or deed, that might lead him into troubled waters or onto dangerous shoals.

So ran the old man's perception of Dick Cheney as his oldest son stood on the brink of entering the presidential lists in the year 1999. It was a misjudgment of character and personality that by comparison would make his choice of Dan Quayle as a vice presidential running mate look like a stroke of genius.

✱ ✱ ✱

"His unique talent, as he recognized early in his career was to convey a sense of soothing solemnity; Cheney could make whatever he said sound so obvious, reasonable and self-evident that listeners often didn't stop to question it."

—JAMES MANN ON DICK CHENEY IN *RISE OF THE VULCANS: THE HISTORY OF BUSH'S WAR CABINET*

What does George-the-father really think about his son's following Dick Cheney's Neo-Con lead and triggering a preemptive war that's led to the erosion of America's power and prestige around the world? Of George W.'s embrace of the Scopes Trial world view of the Theocratic Right? Of the transfer over the last half-decade of presidential power to the Vice President's office, allowing the Prince of Undisclosed Darkness to set and influence policy in virtually every area of executive governance?

As someone who has known and worked with George H. W. Bush for nearly three decades, I've been asked these questions, in one form or another, since the day George W. ordered American troops into Iraq. Even for a longtime friend and observer of the Bushes, both old and young, the answers don't come easily.

Keep in mind, we're not talking about an Oprah Winfrey/Dr. Phil "Let me share my inner feelings" sort of family. In the twenty-nine years I've known them, in politics and out, I can think of only one occasion on which George H. W. and Barbara went into family matters in a revealing way. That related to the death of their daughter Robin at age three from leukemia, and the story was drawn out of them only because we needed it to complete George's 1987 autobiography, *Looking Forward*. (I reflect on that reticence whenever I hear other politicians exploit their family tragedies to elicit sympathy around election time.)

Yet, given the caveat that what happens in the Bush family stays in the Bush family, here's one speechwriter/biographer's read on what George H. W. really thinks about his son's conduct of the presidency he inherited not by Divine Right but from his earth-bound father:

First, the George Bush I knew and worked for in the 1980s would never have supported a foreign policy geared to preemptive war *or* an antiterrorist program that condones torture. For that matter, neither would the George W. Bush I knew when he was Governor of Texas in the 1990s—but that, of course, was before he arrived in Washington and came under the round-the-clock influence of Neo-Con war hawks and Theo-Con Bible thumpers (Dick Cheney being point man for the former, Paul Weyrich for the latter).

In his study of the two Iraq conflicts (*The Wars of the Bushes*), Stephen Tanner speculates that, in effect, George the Elder learned what he knew of his son's decision to invade Iraq from watching CNN; that the old man was shut out of the decision-making process leading up to the invasion by a posturing Harry Hotspur determined to write his own page in history. In large part that remained the conventional wisdom around Washington until Robert Gates' post-election appointment in 2006, though knowing George the Elder's passionate focus on foreign policy, I never for a moment believed it.

For one thing, it would have been difficult if not impossible to have kept a former president/CIA director in the dark about large-scale war preparations in the Middle East. In addition to briefings from both the National Security Council and CIA sources, George H. W., though technically out of government, had high-level contacts in both the State Department (beginning with Secretary of State Colin Powell) and the intelligence community; not to mention contacts with high-level international figures urging him to use his influence to stop the drift toward war.

Their assumption, of course, was that a father who, in addition to his credentials as a former president and diplomat, had actually experienced war would have influence over a son who hadn't; that George W., for all his macho rhetoric, would heed the old man's counsel to wait and see what the UN inspectors came up with on weapons of mass destruction.

The assumption proved wrong. Instead, the son chose to follow the lead of a vice president who, like himself, had "other priorities" when his own time came to serve in Vietnam, though together they had no compunction about putting the lives of young Americans at risk in the volatile killing fields of the Middle East.

Thanks to a flippant *Newsweek* headline ("The Wimp Factor") and Ann Richards's taunting remarks at the Democratic national convention ("Poor George, born with a silver foot in his mouth"), George H. W. Bush entered the 1988 presidential race with an undeserved reputation as a preppy lightweight. In a rational world George might have set matters straight merely by pointing to his record, but the political world is anything but rational and the Washington press corps does not give up its cherished stereotypes easily: Hillary Clinton, no matter how many Liberal issues she plays dodge ball with, will always be pictured as a Leftist flame thrower, and John McCain, no matter how many issues he flip-flops on, will always be Senator Straight Talk.

The stereotype that followed George the Elder throughout his political career was that of a transplanted New England fop who had success handed to him in everything he aimed for. In fact, little of George H. W.'s success had come easily. After serving as a decorated naval aviator in World War II, he could have settled in as a New York stock broker in his father's old firm, but chose instead to move out on his own as an oil equipment salesman in sagebrush country. Entering politics as a Republican in then-overwhelmingly Democratic Texas, he won a seat in Congress but was twice defeated in runs for the U.S. Senate. In the 1970s, two Republican presidents, Nixon and Ford, handed him thankless appointments—national committee chairman during Watergate and CIA director when the agency was under investigation—that would have ended the career of someone less resilient. He not only survived but turned the assignments into building blocks for the future.

Then, of course, to the bafflement of Washington pundits who belittled his candidacy, George, having entered the campaign as a decided underdog, emerged as Ronald Reagan's leading challenger in the 1980 bid for the Republican presidential nomination.

"John Connally was busy in the boardrooms cultivating Wall Street backers," Bush's campaign manager James A. Baker III said at the time, "while George was working Republican caucus voters in Iowa with his sleeves rolled up."

Yet even after winning the Iowa caucus vote and going on to outlast Connally, Howard Baker, Bob Dole, and all other better-known challengers, George H. W. had a hard time getting Reagan's nod as his vice presidential choice. In addition to the Rumsfeld-Kissinger effort to put together a Reagan-Ford ticket, there was the added complication that both the presidential candidate and his wife preferred someone other than George as a running mate. Nancy pushed hard for family friend Senator Paul Laxalt, and Ron had simply bought into the stereotype of George Bush as a New England Brahmin he wouldn't care to know. Only after a one-hour sit-down with Bush to size each other up was Reagan finally persuaded that George H. W.'s taste for pork rinds and the music of Reba McIntire was genuine, not feigned.

By the end of their eight years in office together, Ronald Reagan and George Bush had become close friends and political partners. They enjoyed each other's company at regular Thursday lunch sessions in the White House, sharing common interests and views on everything from political philosophy to the oddities surrounding the social mores of the national capital. The bond surprised some but not those observers who knew both men.

For my part, though heartland conservatives took a jaundiced view of George H. W. because of his Ivy League background, a lasting impression had emerged from our first meeting in the fall of 1964. I was Barry Goldwater's deputy press secretary at the time and George H. W. was a young, energetic Republican county chairman in Houston, wearing a Goldwater button and running for the United States Senate against the Democratic incumbent, Ralph Yarborough. It would be a losing campaign, but in the long run a winner, since Bush's overriding political aim at the time was to build a two-party system in traditionally Democratic Texas—to make the Republican label a credible alternative for Texas voters unhappy with the direction the national Democratic party was moving.

In that, the old man succeeded. By the time his son came along in the mid-'90s, the political playing field in Texas, even against a formidable Democratic rival like Ann Richards, had been made level: Yet another debt owed by George W. to his earth-bound father.

✳ ✳ ✳

In some ways George W. is indeed his father's son: an inexhaustible supply of physical energy that wears out aides is one notable example, an obsession with staying on schedule is another. But the similarity ends with even a cursory look at where the energy goes and what the schedule includes.

In a September 2006 *Vanity Fair* feature on the political Bushes, reporter Todd Purdum worked overtime to make the case that, contrary to conventional wisdom, Bush-41 and Bush-43 are essentially "the same stock in a different box."

A counter-intuitive take on the Bush dynasty but not easy to accept unless you have no problem visualizing George H. W., a genuine combat pilot, being vain (and obtuse) enough to land on an aircraft carrier festooned with a made-for-TV banner reading MISSION ACCOMPLISHED.

No, if Purdum was looking for the Bush son most like his father, he'd have done better to bypass Washington and head south to Tallahassee, Florida.

True, Brother Jeb's physical resemblance to the old man isn't as strong as Dubya's, and he can't work a room with the easy bonhomie of either of the Georges. But beneath these superficial characteristics lie the core values and instincts that set the father apart from other politicians of his era.

In his autobiography, *Looking Forward,* George H. W. tells of the decision he and Barbara arrived at after he finished college "to make it on our own," by rejecting an offer to follow in his father Prescott's footsteps as a New York investment banker. No comfortable man-in-the-grey-flannel-suit life in Greenwich, Connecticut, for young George H. W.. Unlike his privileged peers at Phillips Andover and Yale, he would "break away" to travel to distant Texas, where he and his young wife could "shape our own future."

Compare now the separate career paths taken by the two oldest Bush boys, each destined to reach the higher rungs of American politics: George W., though posing as a rebel, followed family tradition as a third generation legacy at Yale (DKE fraternity, Skull and Bones, like Dad and Granddad), then settled in Texas to build both a business and political career under the sheltering wing of the Bush family escutcheon. Jeb, on the other hand, became the first Bush in three generations to spurn Yale to attend the University of Texas, moving after graduation to Florida, where he could shape his own future as a businessman, then state Secretary of Commerce, and finally as a governor elected on his record rather than his family's name and influence.

Nor does the similarity between George H. W. and his number-two son end there: Jeb, like his father, can be short-tempered without being petulant; can be caught up emotionally at times but never enough to make impulsive shoot-from-the-hip decisions, spending long hours poring over memoranda, reports, and studies on whatever issues are on his desk.

Summing up, to borrow Todd Purdum's phrase, the same stock in a different box...

* * *

"I've learned that leadership isn't just making decisions and giving orders. It's hearing all points of view before making the decision. That's the way leadership works in a free society, by keeping open-door minds. For that matter, it's important everywhere in American life—tolerance for the other person's point of view—understanding that as Americans the values we share are more important than any differences we have."
—GEORGE H. W. BUSH ON PRESIDENTIAL LEADERSHIP, 1989

"I'm going to do what I think is right, and if people don't like me for it, that's just the way it is."
—GEORGE W. BUSH ON PRESIDENTIAL LEADERSHIP, 2006

Working for George the Elder, you soon got the idea that of the two sides of political life, campaigning and governing, he went through the motions in the former but found his true calling in the latter. Not that he didn't put an equal amount of energy into both, but the round-the-clock fund-raising and partisan jousting that go into modern political campaigns were for him a quirky means to a desired end. He would rather have spent his time thinking about and dealing with policy and programs.

Yet another example of like father, unlike son: For young George, as we've witnessed the past six years, the two sides of political life in the White House come together in a seamless view of the president's role as one part Oval Office Decider, the other part Pulpiteering Demagogue. Never, not even during the moving-feast presidency of Bill Clinton, has an American president so lustily embraced the idea of what Norman Ornstein and Thomas Mann have aptly labeled "the permanent campaign." Sleeves rolled, tieless, roving microphone in hand (always before hand-picked audiences), George W. the president and George W. the permanent campaigner have in the past six years been indistinguishable, whether pitching his administration's case for Social Security reform or transforming Iraq into the Switzerland of the Middle East.

For the first two years of George W.'s presidency I saw his hyperactive travel schedule as a calculated White House effort to lift the national spirit after 9/11. But as his extended trips came to match and exceed those of Bill Clinton during Clinton's years in office, I soon concluded that George wasn't on the road so much to reassure the country as to reassure himself of his capacity to lead: To the television-mesmerized generation of the 1950s and '60s, to *be* presidential you have to *look* presidential, and that means lights, cameras, action. Or if not action, activity, which for George W. (like Clinton) is the same thing.

Unlike his father, who thrived on reading reports and firing off memos from the Oval Office, George W. is known to despise routine desk work. Two straight days in the Oval Office and he's chafing to break free, ready to head out the door at the drop of an Air Force One manifest. For the father, a speech—especially a televised speech with its time-consuming rehearsals—was an unwanted, even if necessary, break in the work routine; for the son it *is* the work routine.

Case in point: That Leni Riefenstahl-like staging of a prime-time televised speech in New Orleans' Jackson Square a few weeks after Katrina—the rest of the city was in darkness but at the cost of thousands of taxpayer dollars, special generators were brought in to light up St. Louis Cathedral as a dramatic backdrop. What the White House image polishers were hoping to recreate was Dubya's magic moment amid the rubble of the Twin Towers in September 2001. No bullhorn or firefighters at his side this time, but there he was, the president of the United States on camera, coatless and tieless, *looking* presidential. Aaron Sorkin couldn't have staged it better with Martin Sheen for *The West Wing*.

It was the sort of made-for-television event that George the Elder instinctively rejected as empty-calorie leadership. Bring in the cameras, turn on the lights, hand him a ready-made script, and for some reason the old man would miss his mark, flub his lines, show by his body language that while he was going through the motions, he'd rather be somewhere else: Specifically, back in the Oval Office *being* presidential.

And that he was, right up to the moment he boarded Air Force One that clear, cold day in January 1993 and headed home to Houston. But looking back, I wonder if he ever had second thoughts about not having played the *West Wing* game with the cameras, lights, and made-for-TV scripts. That way, like his son and Bill Clinton, he might have served two terms in the White House instead of only one.

A year later, I visited the former president at his home in Houston and found him preoccupied with what by then had become an expanded family business: not one but two sons running for governorships, a dynastic outreach even Papa Joe Kennedy never dreamed of; though like most political prophets in early 1994, I questioned George W.'s ability to win a general election in Texas over an experienced campaigner like Ann Richards.

Of Jeb's ability to win the Florida governorship, however, I had no doubt. I remembered those rousing speeches he'd made on behalf of his father in the 1980s, heard he was running well in Miami and across Florida, and fully expected that, whatever happened to his older brother in Texas that year, there'd be at least one Bush sworn in as a governor come January 1995.

The story is that on election night, as the numbers poured in assuring his upset victory over Ann Richards, young George turned peevish because his parents, instead of rejoicing over his success, were heard lamenting his younger brother's failure. Looking back, it was a lamentation we all might have joined in: Had Jeb been elected governor of Florida in 1994 rather than four years later, who can doubt—other than the aging Boy Genius, Karl Rove—that he rather than his older brother would have been the Republican presidential nominee in the year 2000 (and would have carried Florida without making a federal case of it)?

And if, by some fortuitous stroke of history, it had in fact been Jeb, not George W., who'd entered the Oval Office as Bush-43 in January 2001, what then? A president, for one, more like his father; which is only to say, the president the American people thought they were getting when they elected his older brother.

* * *

Excerpt from *The New Yorker*, November 20, 2006:
"The day after the election, at a press conference in the East Room of the White House, the curtain rose on Act III of 'Oedipus Bush.' On one level, the current President Bush was all crisp decisiveness as he announced the replacement of his Secretary of Defense, Donald Rumsfeld, with Robert Gates, a former CIA director and the president of Texas A & M University ... Rumsfeld is one of the first President Bush's least favorite people; Gates is one of his most trusted confidants ... At the Pentagon, Rumsfeld yields to Gates; in the Oval Office, adolescent rebellion gives way to sullen acquiescence."

Well, now, it appears that earthbound fathers have something to offer, after all.[1]

---

[1] According to a source familiar with the White House scene at the time, the prime mover behind George W.'s decision to replace Donald Rumsfeld with his father's old friend Robert Gates wasn't Karl Rove or Chief of Staff Josh Bolten, but the president's number one surrogate during the 2006 campaign, Laura Bush. Prior efforts by the First Lady to send Rummy packing proved futile, but when campaign polls showed conduct of the Iraq war to be the main factor moving independent voters toward voting Democratic, even Rummy's chief defender Dick Cheney ran out of reasons to keep him on the job.

Chapter 5

THE IMPERIAL VICE PRESIDENCY

"Men do not change, they unmask themselves."

—Madame de Staël

"My theory is that it's not really Dick but his evil twin brother Mordred."

—Old Cheney congressional colleague

"Seventeen agents?"

"Seventy. Seven-oh."

"For a party in Maryland?"

"Right. About twenty miles outside Washington."

A pause at the other end of the line, then: "Who was the host, Ché Guevara?"

I'd called a retired Secret Service agent—a member of the protective detail during my days as George H. W.

Bush's speechwriter—after getting word that Vice President Dick Cheney had carried no fewer than six dozen bodyguards with him to a waterfront reception on Chesapeake Bay. That's *seventy* armed agents, plus a hovering helicopter, plus three motorized boats circling the waters, in case Osama bin Laden managed to slip one of his fleet of suicide submarines past the Coast Guard to launch a dirty bomb.

Not to minimize the gravity of the terrorist threat, but seventy agents swarming over a private residence to protect the *Vice* President on a Sunday jaunt to the D.C. suburbs seemed a bit excessive. I recalled the evening Ronald Reagan went to a dinner party in northern Virginia with no more than twenty agents on duty—and that came after March 1981, when he was nearly assassinated by John Hinckley.

Clearly, what we've had in Dick Cheney is a high-maintenance vice president with an exaggerated sense of al Qaeda's outreach and/or his own importance. His daily motorcade to the office from the vice president's mansion on Massachusetts Avenue to the Eisenhower Executive Office Building next to the White House—a distance of little more than two miles—consists of anywhere from a dozen to eighteen vehicles, sirens blaring, tying up traffic at the peak of Washington's morning rush hour. The president himself requires only a third that many.

It's all of a pattern, of course, a bizarre manifestation of the full-moon paranoia we first witnessed on 9/11, the day the Vice President gave orders that Air Force One, instead of heading directly back to Washington, route the President to a military bunker in heartland Nebraska.

Following that, there was the disquieting business of the Vice President's need to hunker down each night at some "undisclosed location," while the President himself, oblivious to any black-hooded jihadists snaking through the Rose Garden, had no problem putting in eight hours' sleep at 1600 Pennsylvania Avenue.

Finally, we saw this febrile passion for failsafe security descend to parody when Cheney was nowhere to be seen the night of the 2002 State of the Union address, the stated reason being it was considered high risk, post-9/11, for the President and Vice President to show up in the same building at the same time.

But of course ...

Given the possibility of al Qaeda's slipping past the Army, Navy, Air Force, Secret Service, and FBI to plant a bomb in the U.S. Capitol, we'd need a backup plan: the President, Congress, Cabinet, Supreme Court, and entire foreign diplomatic corps might be in smithereens, but the Republic would stand because, Plan B, somewhere out there (at a location yet to be disclosed) President Cheney would be on the phone, telling Air Force One where to pick him up.

Paranoid Dick, a leader for the times.

* * *

The irony is that when Dick Cheney was named George W. Bush's running mate in the year 2000, he was considered the answer to questions being raised about the presidential candidate's lack of *gravitas*. That, after all, had been

Cheney's strong suit from the day in 1968 he first arrived on Capitol Hill as a congressional intern: an aura, even at age twenty-seven, of gravity. In a chatterer's town like Washington, where talk is cheap and opinion in surplus, a reputation for speaking only when there's something serious to say can carry its owner a long way.

It was in contrast to Newt Gingrich, the rabid partisan he served with in Congress during the 1980s, that Cheney also earned a reputation as a GOP moderate. In a March 1989 report on the Wyoming congressman's surprise appointment as George H. W. Bush's secretary of defense, the *New York Times* described Cheney as "a conservative who is also a compromiser."

"Conservative military analysts drew comfort today from Mr. Cheney's clear conservatism," wrote *Times* reporter Andrew Rosenthal. "Liberals, meanwhile, said the congressman had shown himself not to be bound at all times by his ideology."

"He's an unusual politician, not a back-slapping kind of guy," wrote another correspondent, Morton Kondracke, in the *New Republic*. "As a congressman, Cheney won respect by observing keenly, speaking softly, inventing shrewd stratagems, and sticking to his guns."

That fairly well describes the Dick Cheney people viewed as a steadying influence on George W. Bush when the two came to power a dozen years later: a seasoned, unflappable, Central Casting model of the kind of leader Americans look to in times of crisis.

But buried deep inside a *Washington Post* story written when Cheney took over the Pentagon was another portrait, one painted in darker strokes by an anonymous aide to a Democratic congressman.

"He's able to appear so cool and rational, but there's this other side," the staffer told the *Post*'s Phil McComb. "There was a harshness, that sneer he'd get, attributing bad motives to his opponents—that you were suspect, pro-Communist. There was a venom—he made some very vicious remarks. He scares me."

So it was there all the time. We just hadn't turned to the back pages.

I'd known Cheney's wife Lynne since our years together at *Washingtonian* magazine where we were said to be the only Republicans on the editorial staff. Lynne was a smart, prolific writer-editor with an outgoing personality that belied her background as a PhD who'd written her doctoral thesis on "The Influence of Immanuel Kant on the Poetry of Matthew Arnold."

The Cheneys at the time—the mid-1980s—were regarded as an up-and-coming Washington power couple, though Dick's potential as a national candidate was handicapped by the electoral anemia of his native Wyoming. Still, given the reputation he'd earned for efficiency as both White House chief of staff for Jerry Ford and as a House member, there seemed little doubt he'd be a major Washington player in future years.

Another thing in Dick Cheney's favor, by my lights, was what I saw as an irreverent view of the Washington political scene. For some years I'd been working, with sputtering energy, on a political novel titled *The Body Politic*, based on my experience as press secretary to Vice President Spiro

Agnew in the early 1970s (pre-Watergate and before Agnew's Titanic hit an iceberg). Knowing that Lynne had previously written a novel, I asked if she'd join me as coauthor of a fiction involving a Republican vice president who dies of a heart seizure while in the carnal embrace of a curvaceous television news reporter. She read what I'd written, liked it, and said she'd check it out with Dick. Most congressmen, playing it safe, would have told their wives to confine their literary output to writing recipes for cookbooks. But Dick thought the book had a funny premise that might lead to a movie. With that, a collaboration was born.

The year, keep in mind, was 1986, a decade and a half before a Republican with a heart condition did, indeed, become vice president. That *The Body Politic* attracted more attention after George W. Bush named Dick his vice presidential running mate than it had when first published was understandable, as was Lynne's reluctance to talk about the pivotal sex scene that, she assured reporters, wasn't written by her but by her coauthor.

Indeed it had, along with most of the book, after she left the *Washingtonian* to chair the National Endowment for the Humanities. But without Lynne's input, I doubt the novel would have been finished. Nor would it have drawn the interest of a Hollywood studio attracted by the pitch line, *The Vice President is dead—will anyone notice?*

It's a good line if you were pitching a story to a studio in Hollywood during the 1980s. But today? The old Alexander Throttlebottom/Dan Quayle stereotype of the impotent American vice president has been replaced, irony of ironies, by Dick Cheney's image as a vice president so powerful that he pulls the strings on an empty-saddle cowboy who sits in the Oval Office.

* * *

"Go fuck yourself."

—THE VICE PRESIDENT OF THE UNITED STATES TO THE

SENIOR SENATOR FROM MAINE, JUNE 22, 2004

"I feel better for having said it."

—THE VICE PRESIDENT, REFLECTING TWO DAYS LATER ON HIS SUGGESTION

THAT SENATOR PATRICK LEAHY MONO-COPULATE

(*FOX NEWS*)

What had incited Vice President Cheney's blue-collar eloquence that day was Pat Leahy raising questions about the number of no-bid multibillion-dollar contracts awarded the Halliburton company in Iraq.

Any implication that because he was formerly CEO of Halliburton he'd helped influence the Department of Defense in awarding those contracts was, said Cheney, "an attack on my integrity." For Leahy or anyone else to make such insinuations without evidence to back them up was, according to the Vice President, "reprehensible."

Leahy, for his part, wondered how any evidence about Halliburton's dealings with DOD could be produced, since then-Secretary Rumsfeld refused to release copies of any document concerning the contracts: *Executive privilege, classified information, whatever... You want copies? Here's my answer: Go...*

Don Rumsfeld and Dick Cheney—two cuts from the same Machiavellian cloth, each, as Shakespeare's Richard III said of Buckingham, his "other self." In the beginning it was Rumsfeld as mentor, putting the quick-learning Cheney on his congressional staff and bringing him along when the call came from Richard Nixon to head up the Office of Economic Development (Nixon obviously seeing something of *his* "other self" in young Congressman Rumsfeld); then on to the Ford White House, where a pliant president, overwhelmed by his office, was only too glad to delegate nut-cutting duties to two bright, energetic power players who not only carried them out but did so with gusto.

So it was that when Brent Scowcroft, who had been Ford's NSC Director, told the *New Yorker* in October 2005 that although he'd known Dick Cheney for thirty years, "I don't know Dick Cheney now," I had to wonder what Scowcroft was doing in the Ford White House when the Rumsfeld-Cheney team engineered their defenestrating Halloween Massacre in the fall of 1975. With one swift stroke, Rumsfeld, the president's chief of staff, and Cheney, his deputy, dispatched, via forced resignation or outright firing, the vice president, two Cabinet members, and the director of the Central Intelligence Agency.

In the vice president's case, Nelson Rockefeller was simply advised that unless he announced his disinterest in renomination, the president would unceremoniously dump him at the national convention in Kansas City. Rockefeller's sin: overstepping his bounds as vice president.

"In the Ford Administration, we had major problems in managing the vice presidential relationship," Cheney later told a *Washington Monthly* forum, going on to describe how Rockefeller not only tried to involve himself in foreign affairs but also had the chutzpah to come forward with "plans to address health care, education, and economic issues."

Somebody obviously had to put Rockefeller in his place, to see to it that his plans were shot down before they reached the president's desk: "I was the SOB," Cheney told his audience, "and on a number of occasions got involved in shouting matches with the vice president."

And what's more, felt better for having done it.

The ostensible purpose of the Halloween Massacre was to reinforce Gerald Ford's right flank as he prepared to do battle with California's Ronald Reagan for the Republican presidential nomination. Dumping Nelson Rockefeller, the Political Enemy Number One for Goldwater conservatives, was a giant step in that direction. But there were other moves made by the Rumsfeld-Cheney team that hinted at another, more personal agenda.

With Rockefeller on his way out, an opening came clear for some ticket-balancing Republican politician to serve as Ford's vice presidential running mate the following year. An obvious choice would have been George Herbert Walker Bush, the popular former congressman, U.N. ambassador, and Republican National Committee chairman who'd been a close runner-up when Ford picked Rockefeller for the vice presidency a year before. But Donald Rumsfeld had other ideas.

Rumsfeld and Bush had served in the House together during the mid-'60s. Rumsfeld, from Illinois, and Bush, the Texas/New Englander, were both viewed by Richard Nixon as rising political stars, the future of the Republican party. Both would play a role in the Nixon administration, Rumsfeld as head of the Office of Economic Development, Bush in the more prestigious roles of U.S. ambassador to the United Nations and chairman of the Republican National Committee.

For Bush, whose background and instincts led him to shun political in-fighting, there was no thought given to any possible rivalry with the onetime congressional colleague he knew as "Rummy." Rumsfeld, however, saw their relationship differently. The White House chief of staff had national political ambitions and (unlike Bush) was ready, willing, and eager to cut down anything and anybody that stood in his way.

Bush, in Beijing as the Ford administration's envoy to China, got word of the shake-up in Washington via orders to return home for a new assignment. There were two possibilities: secretary of commerce, a Cabinet post being vacated by Rogers Morton, or CIA director, a radioactive position being vacated by William Colby. The Commerce job, an ideal fit given Bush's business background, would have set him up for the vice presidential nomination, while the CIA, with the agency under investigation by two congressional committees, was the last place in government anyone with political aspirations would want to be; which is exactly where Rumsfeld, quoted as wanting to "bury the sonofabitch," placed Bush.

"I think you ought to know what people up here are saying about your going to the CIA," another former House colleague told George H. W. Bush shortly after he arrived back in Washington. "They feel you've been had, George. Rumsfeld set you up, and you were a damned fool to take the job."

Whatever dark thoughts George H. W. had about being set up, he swallowed his resentment and went on to handle his CIA assignment in a way that, much to Rumsfeld's chagrin, turned it into a political asset in the years that followed.

A quarter-century later, Rummy's calculated attempt to bury George the Elder would rise in Bush family memory, a wall blocking his return to power as George W. Bush's secretary of defense. It would take the most persuasive effort of Rumsfeld's onetime protégé, Dick Cheney, to tear the wall down.

Dick and Rummy: Together Again

As a political family, the Bushes are known for the premium they place on loyalty, and in the case of the Bush offspring, a long memory for those who did, or tried to do, harm to the old man. For the eldest of the Bush boys, despite any differences he might have had with his father over the years, the strain ran deep.

"The sonofabitch tried to kill my father," George W. told Democratic Senate leader Tom Daschle in the days leading up to the Iraq war. That, as far as young George was concerned, was reason enough to take out Saddam Hussein, WMDs or no WMDs.

At a less-heated level of personal animus, George W. also kept a mental list of those political malefactors he regarded as fitting subjects for political payback. High on the list was the back-room political conniver who had not only screwed the old man out of the vice presidency in 1976, but tried to do it again at the Republican convention in 1980. Rumsfeld, the Bushes knew, was a key member of the cabal that worked unsuccessfully to cobble together a Reagan-Ford ticket that year, despite the fact that George H. W., as runner-up to Reagan in the delegate count, was the obvious vice presidential choice.

That Dick Cheney himself hadn't been tainted by his association with Rumsfeld was due to the independent credentials he'd earned as Wyoming's at-large congressman after leaving the White House. Alan Simpson, the state's senior senator, happened to be one of George H. W. Bush's closest friends in Washington, and it was with Simpson's recommendation that Bush appointed Cheney Secretary of Defense in 1989, after Bush's first choice, John Tower, had been rejected by the Senate. Another key Cheney booster: Secretary of State James Baker, whose first break in national politics had come when Cheney put him in charge of the Ford presidential campaign in 1976.

It was as Secretary of Defense during the first Gulf War that Cheney emerged as one-half of the two-man team of military planners charged with carrying out George H. W.'s pledge to drive Saddam Hussein out of Kuwait and caponize the Iraqi dictator's threat to his Middle East neighbors. Along with Colin Powell, Chairman of the Joint Chiefs of Staff, the grounded, soft-spoken secretary became a familiar figure in American homes. When the war came to a swift, successful conclusion, Cheney's future as a man to be reckoned with in national affairs was assured.

Cheney-Powell proved a winning team that George H. W. Bush was unabashedly proud of having put together. The introverted Secretary and outgoing General seemed perfectly matched, not only to carry out a war but also to sell it to a nation understandably gun-shy after the Vietnam experience of two decades earlier.

There was only one problem with this picture: Dick and Colin didn't much like each other. Cheney considered Powell an overreaching publicity hound, a man who spent too much time talking to Bob Woodward to be trusted. Powell saw Cheney as a man who, not having experienced war, was given to grandiose military-geopolitical projects that played well in war games, but played hell in actual war.

What especially galled Cheney was his inability to counter the charismatic Powell's influence with the President when policy differences developed. "Operation Scorpion," for example, was a plan conceived by the Secretary of Defense and his war hawk deputy, Paul Wolfowitz, to destabilize Saddam's regime by stationing U.S. troops outside Baghdad. Brilliant plan, computer-tested, but shot down when Powell convinced Bush that any prolonged occupation of Iraq by foreign forces could prove disastrous.

Eleven years later, on the cusp of returning to power as vice president, Dick Cheney viewed that failure to take out Saddam as unfinished business, a blemish on his resume. Hell-bent on seeing to it that this time around Powell, the incoming Secretary of State, would be boxed in, Cheney set about to place a kindred spirit in charge at Defense, a seasoned Washington power-player he could rely on in the White House turf wars that lay ahead.

Dick knew just the man, though it would be no easy job to get him past George W.: The sonofabitch, after all, had tried to bury his father.

* * *

"White House Chief of Staff Donald Rumsfeld had a reputation as a skillful political in-fighter. It was inevitable that he'd be singled out in any rumor having to do with engineering my move to the CIA.

In a meeting in his office, Rumsfeld vehemently denied the rumor.

I accepted his word."

—GEORGE H. W. BUSH, IN HIS AUTOBIOGRAPHY, *LOOKING FORWARD*

The U.S. military, argued the Bush-Cheney campaign in 2000, had been run into the ground by eight years of benign neglect under Bill Clinton. To rebuild it, Cheney now told young Bush, a strong, experienced hand was needed at Defense to upgrade and streamline America's armed forces for the 21st century. There were unseen threats to our national security out there, enemies of freedom and all Old Glory stands for.

That was the easy part of the sell: Getting young George to see himself as the second coming of Franklin D. Roosevelt and John F. Kennedy, a president chosen by God to lead his country in a time of peril, was a piece of cake. Working Rumsfeld into the cake mix was another matter—a ploy requiring all the manipulative skills Cheney (and Rumsfeld) had learned pulling Gerald Ford's strings three decades earlier.

First would come the charade of compiling a list of possible DOD appointees, an exercise not unlike the one Cheney had practiced in the lead-up to George's choice of a running mate. Names tossed around for DOD during sessions at Bush's Crawford, Texas, ranch included Senator John Warner, Paul Wolfowitz, and former Senator Sam Nunn, none of whom, for one reason or another, met Cheney's standard as the man Bush needed to work his executive will at the Pentagon (Warner wouldn't want the job; Wolfowitz was an abrasive policy grind who wouldn't go over well on Capitol Hill; Nunn was a retiree who'd been out of touch).

The trick was to persuade young George to meet with Rumsfeld, then decide whether the sins of the past should cloud his judgment on the needs of the present. Get them one on one in a room, then on a grand tour of the ranch, and all things were possible.

Don Rumsfeld, for all his public persona as a gelid-eyed, jut-jawed Prussian, could be a charmer when it suited his purpose. In his all-day meetings with the president-elect at Crawford, Rummy was more on his game than at any time since he interviewed with Richard Nixon thirty years before, for his breakthrough appointment as head of Nixon's Office of Economic Opportunity. The buttons to push were obvious: How could young George possibly turn down an über-macho Princeton man who'd flown fighter planes (albeit peacetime) as an aviator for the God Almighty Marines? Plus the fact that Rummy, a misplaced leather-booted Texan if the president-elect ever saw one, shared Dubya's bilious feelings about Liberals, the Eastern media, and Washington in general.

In twenty-four hours, as Cheney had hoped, the deal was closed: Dick and Don were together again. And Colin Powell?

Excerpt, *Associated Press* report, December 17, 2005:

Speaking to reporters in London, former Secretary of State Colin L. Powell accused Defense Secretary Donald H. Rumsfeld and Vice President Cheney of cutting him out of key decisions and going behind his back directly to President Bush before the U.S.-led invasion in 2003. "Very often, Mr. Rumsfeld and Vice President Cheney would take decisions in to the President that the rest of us weren't aware of," Powell said. "That happened on a number of occasions."

Cheney's Cheney

Priorities

On the morning of January 22, 2001, his first day on the job as Vice President Dick Cheney's chief of staff, I. Lewis (Scooter) Libby placed a priority phone call, via the White House switchboard (American taxpayers' expense), to Marc Rich, one of Libby's former legal clients then living in Bern, Switzerland. It was a congratulatory call triggered by Rich's having finally, after the expenditure of tens of millions of dollars in thinly disguised bribes, been granted a full presidential pardon for crimes involving fraud, defalcation, and dirty-money laundering—not to mention fleeing the country and earning a special niche among the FBI's most-wanted white-collar fugitives from justice.

In the days preceding Libby's priority call, news of Bill Clinton's egregious pardon of fugitive Rich had brought on torrents of editorial condemnation coast to coast. The national feeling was summed up by an eye-rolling Midwestern congressman who branded it "one last example of Bill Clinton's outrageous abuse of the power and prestige of the presidency."

It was exactly the sort of tawdry access-for-money political deal the Bush-Cheney campaign had railed against in 2004, promising clean government and a return to morality and family values in the White House.

Given that background, Libby's personal call to his felonious ex-client Marc Rich was a harbinger of what we would come to expect from America's first imperial vice presidency: a cynical contempt for ethical standards, an arrogant sense of entitlement, and an all-too-eager readiness to push the limits of power and privilege beyond anything known in Washington since the Office of Vice President was reorganized as an executive adjunct over half a century ago.

To gauge the extent of Dick Cheney's transformation after assuming that office—the toxic mixture of megalomania and paranoia that baffles old friends like Brent Scowcroft—try visualizing any previous vice president playing the Cheney hand: Vice President Walter Mondale taking weekly trips to Langley to spin CIA intelligence; Vice President George H. W. Bush shuttling to Capitol Hill to lecture lawmakers on the virtues of torture and wire-tapping; Vice President Al Gore assembling a task force to draft an energy bill, then telling any and all who want to know the task force roster to go fuck themselves. Or any of the above dispatching his legal advisor (in Cheney's case, David Addington, who would succeed Libby as chief of staff) to tell the White House itself as much when the president's own national security advisors objected to plans to wiretap American citizens.

And what does all this say of the man who sits in the Oval Office—on the rare days, that is, when Dubya is actually in the office and not aboard Air Force One, strutting across the countryside like a wind-up presidential bobblehead, soaking up applause before audiences preselected to stroke his ego? Simply this: For all the Rove-built façade of his being a "strong" chief executive, George W. Bush has been, by comparison to even hapless Jimmy Carter, the weakest, most out-of-touch

American president in modern times. Think Dan Quayle in cowboy boots.

As for Scooter Libby, in his flush years as Cheney's chief of staff—from the morning of his phone call to Marc Rich to the afternoon he was indicted for obstruction of justice in the Valerie Plame case—the diminutive Philadelphia lawyer with a penchant for high living and obscure poetry served as the vice president's shadow at Cabinet meetings, his hammer in dealing with obdurate White House aides, and his monitor on federal contracts moving in and out of Iraq. He was, in short, Cheney's Cheney, and to view Scooter Libby's serpentine role in the Plame affair as Libby acting on his own is to look back in history and believe that H. R. Haldeman was acting on his own, with Richard Nixon in the dark about the Watergate burglary and cover-up.

Dick Cheney as Dick Nixon on andro, George W. Bush as a president on strings. No wonder Brent Scowcroft worries: A vice president in control is bad enough. Worse yet is a vice president out of control.

Chapter 6

A LEAF FLEW IN THE WINDOW

"I get up every morning and worry about protecting the American people."
—Donald Rumsfeld, quoted in the *Washington Post*, April 18, 2006

I N James Mann's *Rise of the Vulcans: The History of Bush's War Cabinet*, we're told why George W. Bush's foreign policy team named itself after the Roman god of fire and the forge: Condoleezza Rice, one of the few carryovers from George the Elder's administration, is from Birmingham, Alabama, as were the wives of two other team members, Colin Powell's Alma and Richard Armitage's Laura.

Birmingham was founded in 1875 as a steel-making town and its highest point, I learned soon after moving there in the early 1950s, is atop Red Mountain. There, brandishing a cone-shaped electric light, stands a fifty-six-foot statue of Vulcan. An inelegant statue by design since, according to Roman mythology, Vulcan was cast out of the heavens because of his ugliness.

Not a problem for Condi and her fellow Vulcanites; in fact, just what the spin doctor ordered because, as Mann points out, the sobriquet "Vulcan" captured perfectly "the image the Bush team sought to convey, a sense of power, toughness, resilience, and durability."

Hardly the image one would expect from the global strategy team of a president whose inaugural address spoke in terms of "humility" and renounced "arrogance" in America's relations with the world. But the gap between George W. Bush's rhetoric and actions in carrying out U.S. foreign policy would only grow in the years that followed. Even as his Pentecostal speechwriter Michael Gerson was reworking drafts of the new president's first State of the Union speech, the Vulcanites, behind the scenes, were sketching out Iraq invasion plans on Pentagon spread-sheets; not surprising in that no fewer than three members of the team—Donald Rumsfeld, Paul Wolfowitz, and Armitage—were cosigners of the 1998 Neo-Con letter to Bill Clinton calling for "regime change" in Baghdad.

Clinton, of course, wasn't receptive to any new initiatives along that line at that particular time. Not only did he have his hands full with a Republican Congress trying to remove him from office, but at Madeleine Albright's urging he was already neck deep into regime change and nation building in the fractious Balkans. To the extent that the Clinton White House paid any attention at all to the Neo-Con letter, it was recognized for what it was—an attempt by its authors to lay down the guidelines for a Middle East foreign policy debate within the Republican party in the period leading up to the 2000 presidential election.

That the letter to Clinton served its long-range purpose was borne out by the pervasive influence of Neo-Con operatives in shaping Middle East policy for the new Bush White House. Surrounded by true believers in the idea that peace in that area hinged on removing Saddam from power, George W.'s campaign pledge to resist foreign policy ventures in nation building didn't survive his first month in office.

There would be regime change in Iraq. All that the Neo-Con war hawks, in the Bush administration and out, needed to bring it about was an excuse to invade. Looking back a half-decade and knowing what we now know, who can doubt that if al Qaeda hadn't obliged the Neo-Cons with 9/11, the Kristolites would have torn a page out of history and, with Rupert Murdoch playing the role of William Randolph Hearst, given us a reprise of the sinking of the Maine?

What forty-and-under readers need to know is that until recent years the Republican party was anything but the party of war hawks. National defense hawks, yes: President Eisenhower's cautionary words about "the military-industrial complex" have largely been ignored by GOP lawmakers whenever the Pentagon comes calling.

But as to committing American troops to battle overseas, until George H. W. Bush ordered the invasion of Iraq in 1991, no Republican president since William McKinley in 1898 had initiated a war; nor, until Richard Nixon in 1969, had any Republican president opted to carry on a war initiated by a Democratic president.

The conservative view, tracing back to a Republican Senate's rejection of Woodrow Wilson's League of Nations treaty in 1919, is that even if George Washington's warning against "foreign entanglements" is impracticable in today's world, the Wilsonian vision of the United States as peace-keeper for the planet is the road to imperial ruin and war without end.

That view, as we know, runs counter to the version of history laid out by patellar Liberal pedagogues Arthur Schlesinger (both Senior and Junior) who hold that but for "a little group of willful men" blocking Senate approval of the League, world peace and harmony would have reigned through the 20th century, the "willful group," as Wilson described them, being Senate Republicans led by Majority Leader Henry Cabot Lodge.

So goes the politically correct line Americans have been taught from grade school through graduate school since the mid-1920s. But Lodge, as World War I historian Thomas Fleming tells us in *The Illusion of Victory*, was "willful" only in that he held to a "conservative philosophy rooted in the Constitution," which led him to object to a treaty that would "oblige the United States to fight foreign wars at the behest of the League of Nations."

Wilson's stiff-necked response to Lodge was that those who opposed the League did so out of "downright ignorance," if not some sinister personal motive. It was typical of the pietistic Princeton don of whom the French premier Georges Clemenceau said, after the Versailles conference, "Talking to Wilson was something like talking to Jesus Christ."

An apt description in that the sanctimonious American president at Versailles in 1919, like the moralizing Neo-Con now in the White House, considered his country's role in the world a mission to democratize, on the order of France's self-perceived "mission to civilize" that sent French armies to four continents in the 18th and 19th centuries: Missions from God, no less, inspired by the hubris that their countries were exceptional in the eyes of the Almighty.

Whether such transcendent notions penetrated the armor-plated psyches of Dick Cheney and Donald Rumsfeld as they plotted the invasion of Iraq is open to question. The vice president and his technocratic soul mate in the Pentagon have never been known to take calls from a higher father. It's sufficient for their purpose that the evangelical urban cowboy in the Oval Office does hear voices in the night. Knowing that, they can play off his moralistic self-image to get their plans approved and the troop ships moving.

Of the half-dozen Vulcanites James Mann focuses on in his study of the Bush-II war cabinet, four were card-carrying

Neo-Cons committed to "regime change" in Iraq years
before 9/11 as well as to the idea that Saddam might be
stockpiling weapons of mass destruction for a Saladin-like
march across the Middle East. The committed—Cheney,
Rumsfeld, Wolfowitz, and Armitage—were unambivalent
in their aims and relentless in their push toward war, with
or without international approval. Outnumbered in the
Situation Room and outgunned in the Oval Office, the
remaining two, Colin Powell and Condoleezza Rice, had
little or no chance to stop what another inside observer
called "the Cheney steamroller."

Or did they?

Washington has its closed circle of Teflon personalities
who aren't held to the same standard of accountability the
national media require of others. Conservatives think of
this double standard as favoring only liberal Democrats
but, in fact, for reasons having to do with the bitch-god-
dess Celebrity, select Republicans fall within the circle.

John McCain can tell a repulsive sex-related joke
about Hillary Clinton and Janet Reno that has guests at
a GOP fund-raiser walking out in disgust, yet doesn't pay
a price for it because he cultivates reporters as if they were
New Hampshire voters. Colin Powell can play a central
role in launching a disastrous war, yet escapes blame for
the consequences because he's spent the better part of two
decades cultivating the image of a compassionate general
surrounded by warmongering civilians (see Woodward's
The Commanders).

To be sure, give Powell his due for warning George H.
W. in 1991 that a march to Baghdad (as was then being

urged by Neo-Con drumbeaters like Richard Perle) would lead the United States into a Vietnam-like quagmire. Give him credit, too, for trying, however fecklessly, to counter the influence of a war-bent vice president who in 2001 saw a march to Baghdad as a cakewalk, with flowers strewn in the path of American troops along the way.

But that said, let's not wipe the slate clean of the indispensable role Powell played in the Bush administration's propaganda campaign to justify the first preemptive war in American history: No member of the Bush administration except Colin Powell could have sold the American people on the Cheney-Rumsfeld-Ahmed Chalabi line that Saddam Hussein was stockpiling chemical and biological weapons, and that unless immediate action was taken, the United States would, in Cheney's words, "become the target of those activities."

The February 2003 image of Powell earnestly making the Bush administration's case that Saddam Hussein was harboring weapons of mass destruction is one the former Secretary of State would have us forget, or at least forgive, based on his having been misled by flawed intelligence given him by CIA Director George Tenet.

Freeze frame. Let's look at that claim a little more closely: We're asked to believe that a battle-tested four-star general, with years of experience dissecting intelligence reports, was snookered in a political exercise he knew full well was being manipulated by a vice president who had worn a path to CIA headquarters in order to arm-twist agents into giving him the "intelligence" he wanted.

But phony CIA data aside, what exactly did Colin Powell expect to accomplish by going before the UN Security Council to make the case for a war he didn't believe in? His apologists explain his conduct by saying he simply put his personal feelings aside and acted the part of the good soldier. Yet consider: In every past instance involving America's role in an international crisis since the UN was founded, the U.S. ambassador, not the secretary of state, was called on to make the country's case.

- In 1950, it was Ambassador Warren Austin, not Secretary of State Dean Acheson, who addressed the Security Council during the Korean war crisis.

- In 1956, it was Ambassador Henry Cabot Lodge, not Secretary of State John Foster Dulles, who spoke for the United States during the Suez Crisis.

- In 1962, it was Ambassador Adlai Stevenson, not Secretary of State Dean Rusk, who presented the country's case during the Cuban Missile Crisis.

- During the Nixon years, it was Ambassador Daniel Patrick Moynihan, not William Rogers or Henry Kissinger, we saw speaking for the United States at critical points in the Vietnam War.

Surely Powell, as good a War College scholar as he is a West Point soldier, knew that history. He also had to know that the only reason the Bush White House would ask him, rather than Ambassador John Negroponte, to address the Security Council that day in February 2003 was to give credibility—credibility no one else in the administration could provide—to its shaky case for war.

In short, the self-advertised "moderate," supposedly waging the good fight against our saber-rattling vice president, let himself be used. As a result, millions of Americans who distrusted the Bush administration but trusted Colin Powell—including skeptics like columnist Mary McGrory—came to believe Iraq possessed weapons of mass destruction, and fell into lockstep with the Vulcanites and their plan to march to Baghdad, with or without multinational support.

What could Powell have been thinking? What possible motive could he have had for letting himself be used by a White House that had frozen him out of its inner circle of policy makers? That's a mystery second only to what George the Elder really thinks of his son's reckless conduct of American foreign policy.

The same can't be said, however, of Condoleezza Rice's enabling role in George W.'s decision to go to war. There's no mystery there: In Condi's case, shilling the Neo-Con argument for regime change in Iraq came as easily and expediently as you'd expect of a Washington careerist with eyes fixed on the next rung up the political ladder.

Working as Brent Scowcroft's NSC deputy in the Bush-41 White House, Rice used her academic expertise to push enthusiastically for her bosses' geopolitical "realist" approach to American engagement overseas. But with Neo-Conservative influence dominant in the Bush-43

White House, a remodeled Condi made her appearance as a regime-changing, nation-building Wilsonian visionary who would urge preemptive action against Saddam because of his stockpiling of aluminum tubes to enrich uranium "for nuclear weapons programs."

"We don't want the smoking gun to be a mushroom cloud," Condi told a CNN audience in September 2002. Her new bosses, Bush-43 and Dick Cheney, had to be pleased. But did Condoleezza Rice—Phi Beta Kappa, summa cum laude, PhD, Stanford Provost, author, linguist, accomplished pianist, Renaissance prodigy—really believe what she was saying? If so, it wouldn't be the first time a beautiful mind in Washington was blinded by sheer ambition.

* * *

Unseen Pachyderms, Silent Hounds

Two animal metaphors came to mind whenever I heard talk of Saddam Hussein's nonexistent weapons of mass destruction. The first was the elephant in the room; the second, Sherlock Holmes' dog that didn't bark.

The elephant in the room was Israel. You don't have to own a doctorate in foreign studies like Condoleezza Rice or be an intellectual mastodon like Charles Krauthammer to know that if Dick Cheney was telling the truth about Iraq's harboring WMDs in 2001, the

Israeli government wouldn't have waited for UN approval before doing something drastic about it.

The same could be said of the dog that didn't bark: That would be what Israeli intelligence had to say on the subject of "yellow-cake," aluminum tubes to enrich uranium, and the threat of Saddam's WMD being, in Dick Cheney's memorable word, "imminent." I wasn't the only curious skeptic who wondered why the Bush-Cheney White House repeatedly cited findings from British, French, German, and Italian intelligence, but never Mossad. Could it have been for the same reason Cheney didn't want to wait for the UN inspectors' report before launching his war? That we might have learned something Big Brother at his Undisclosed Location didn't want us to know?

* * *

It's the Old Man's Fault

"While Saddam Hussein had nothing to do with the actual attacks on America, Saddam Hussein's Iraq was a part of the Middle East that was festering and unstable and part of the circumstances that created the problem on September 11."

—CONDOLEEZZA RICE AT A BUSH-CHENEY CAMPAIGN RALLY, PITTSBURGH, PENNSYLVANIA, OCTOBER 2004

For the triumphalist Vulcans, planning the preemptive war against Saddam's Iraq was easy. (It would, after all, be a cakewalk.) Selling it to the American public would be harder. Short of *Maine* sinkings and Pearl Harbors,

Americans are not an easy people to plunge into foreign wars. Had it not been for 9/11, the Bush White House, determined to go to war, would no doubt have seized on some synthetic provocation, on the order of the one LBJ used to push through the Gulf of Tonkin Resolution in 1965. (It would be déjà vu for all the elder Neo-Cons who, after all, were Johnson Democrats at the time.)

Still, sending American troops into Iraq to avenge the 9/11 bombings remained a hard sell, since the record was fairly clear that far from being allies in the war against the Great Satan, Osama and Saddam despised each other—to the extent, it's fair to say, that, second only to bringing down the Twin Towers and the Pentagon, Osama would have dearly loved to level Saddam's palaces in the Sunni Triangle.

How to paper over the fact that fundamentalist Osama and secular Saddam weren't one-and-the-same enemy would be an ongoing challenge for the Vulcanites and their White House spinmeisters. Floating a report that before 9/11 the head suicide bomber had secretly met in Prague with Saddam's intelligence chief was a starter, but to the consternation of the spinmeisters it was shot down by the CIA. Sending popular administration spokesmen like Condoleezza Rice to rallies to convince the Republican base was another stratagem, but ethical sticklers were quick to point out that National Security Advisors aren't supposed to show up in public as political hacks (to do so privately, like Clinton's Sandy Berger, is another matter).

That left the ultimate sales job to the ultimate salesman in any administration, the President/Commander-in-Chief. It was a role—wartime leader!—that George W. believed he was born again to play, and his first and most important sales pitch would come in his State of the Union speech, January 29, 2002.

In his literary self-celebration of having served as a White House speechwriter (*The Right Man: The Surprise Presidency of George W. Bush*), the Yale-Harvard don David Frum[1] gave the democratized world a detailed rundown—some would say exposé—of how that address was put together: an inside account that to this tired old (Bush-41) speechwriter's eyes could pass for something out of a Joseph Heller satire or Saturday Night Live skit. But judge for yourself...

Excerpt, *The Right Man,* Chapter 12:

"Here's an assignment. Can you sum up in a sentence or two our best case for going after Iraq?"

It was late December 2001 and Mike Gerson was

---

[1] Nothing personal. Just an apt description of a certain type of intellectual functionary found in abundance around the Neo-Conservative Bush White House. Ironic since conservatives found fault with the "double-domed, ivory-tower theorists" (i.e., Yale-Harvard ideologues) in the West Wing of the Kennedy White House during the 1960s. Once again conservatives of that era (like the author) find ourselves peering through the window only to find (Pogo-like) that *We have met the enemy and they is us.* Of the White House ideologues in the Kennedy White House, the sage Democratic House Speaker at the time, Sam Rayburn, famously said, "I only wish one of them had ever run for sheriff." Applied to the Neo-Con noncombatants in the Bush White House, the line would read, "I only wish one of them had ever worn an active-duty uniform."

parceling out the components of the forthcoming State of the Union speech. His request to me could not have been simpler: I was to provide a justification for a war.

Freeze Frame

Not to throw ice water on the happy-day flippancy of a younger generation, but what Gerson and Frum are talking about here is the prospect of sending 150,000 Americans into a war against a vicious regime known to have used chemical weapons in its war against Iran: *One hundred-fifty-thousand American lives at risk, not to mention the unknown consequences of our having launched their "justified" war preemptively...*

Tell me, am I just being a septuagenarian crank or do the words of our president's chief speechwriter, Mike Gerson ("Can you sum up in a sentence or two our best case for going after Iraq?") elicit the same thought in your mind that it did in mine; namely, I'd like to pick both these arrogant noncombatants up by the seat of their Brooks Brothers pants, throw a khaki uniform on them, hand them each an M-4, and ship *them* overseas to "go after Iraq."

But wait: Frum's SNL skit only *begins* with Gerson's let's-do-a-war throwaway line at a West Wing water cooler. Handed the fun job of justifying a war (so much more interesting than justifying a deficit), our hero—I see Bill Murray playing Frum, with Dan Ackroyd as Gerson—cancels lunch in the White House mess, rolls up his French-cuffed shirtsleeves, and goes to work...

Excerpt, *The Right Man*, Chapter 12:

I began pulling books off the shelves. I reread a speech that I had last read on September 11 itself: Roosevelt's "date that will live in infamy" speech. On December 8, 1941, Roosevelt had exactly the same problem we had. The United States had been attacked by Japan, but the greater threat came from Nazi Germany…

Ah, yes, that steel-trap Ivy League mind at work. The parallel's there, don't you see? On September 11, 2001, the United States was actually attacked by al Qaeda, but the greater threat came from Saddam's Iraq.

The more I thought about it the more the relationship between the terror organizations and the terror states resembled the Tokyo-Rome-Berlin Axis…Together, the terror states and the terror organizations formed an axis of hatred against the United States. The United States could not wait for these dangerous regimes to get deadly weapons and attack us; the United States must strike first and protect the world from them.

Enter now (page 237) Condoleezza Rice—think Whoopie Goldberg playing the role—to say that roughing up Saddam was fine, but what about Iran? Why mollycoddle the mullahs? If we're going to shake up the Middle East, let's not go about it in a half-assed way. Then comes Gerson again (top, page 238), satisfied with the Pearl Harbor analogy but not quite happy with "the axis of hatred." The Pentecostal in him says it should be the "axis of *evil*." (I can hear Ackroyd explaining "We're on a mission from God.") Then, finally, (bottom, page 238) someone (Karen Hughes as played by Jane Curtin) steps in to say, "Hey, it takes three to make an axis. Throw in North Korea..."

At which point, Frum's role at an end, the joke becomes reality:

Excerpt, George W. Bush's State of the Union address, January 29, 2002:

States like these, and their terrorist allies, constitute an axis of evil, arming to threaten the peace of the world. By seeking weapons of mass destruction, these regimes pose a grave and growing danger. They could provide these arms to terrorists, giving them the means to match their hatred. They could attack our allies or attempt to blackmail the United States. In any of these cases, the price of indifference would be catastrophic...

I will not wait on events, while dangers gather. I will not stand by, as peril draws closer and closer. The United States of America will not permit the world's most dangerous regimes to threaten us with the world's most destructive weapons.

Sustained applause, cheering.

For David Frum, it was Mission accomplished, time to break out the Dom Perignon. A few weeks later the author of the "axis of evil" speech would leave the White House for a bulletproof position with a Neo-Con think tank. And, of course, go on to profit off his presidential speech-writing experience by writing a self-inflating book. As far as he and his Neo-Con kind were concerned, it was all over but the shooting.

By other people, needless to say.

* * *

Yet, for all that—intelligence leaks, Condi on the stump, the wartime leader invoking the threat of an "axis of evil"—the sale remained up in the air.

Frustrating for a White House accustomed to having its way, but five years of false promise and hubristic bullshit—from "cakewalk" to MISSION ACCOMPLISHED to "Last Throes"—had taken its toll on public confidence and the leader's credibility.

Nothing left to do then, other than (1) borrow a page from the old Vietnam playbook by questioning the patriotism of the media and critics of the war (Rumsfeld: "They're spreading myths and distortions about our troops and our country") and (2) play the ultimate card by laying everything at the feet of the preceding president or, in Dubya's case, his predecessor-once-removed.

In other words, blame the old man.

The reason 9/11 occurred at all, said White House Press Secretary Tony Snow in several hundred ill-chosen words, mid-August of 2006, is that bin Laden was encouraged by our not having finished off Saddam in 1991. It showed we lacked the will, etc., ad nauseum.

Dick Cheney's hand was, for sure, still chafing because he lost that battle in the Oval Office a decade and a half before, when the then-commander in chief refused to march to Baghdad. But the question does remain—how could George W. have approved an official White House statement that placed the fault for the loss of over twenty-three hundred American lives on his own father?

I spent an afternoon thinking that one over, first wondering how the old man took it, then about the way the Bush White House really operates, behind the strutting image of the Decider. And a story came to mind out of my Louisiana youth...

Back in the early 1930s, when Huey Long was still around, we had a governor, O. K. Allen ("It's O.K. with O.K.") who very much looked and strutted like a governor but behind the façade was a smiling dimwit manipulated by, as Huey called himself, the Kingfish. So manipulated, in fact, that Huey's younger brother Earl, when asked to sum up the extent of O.K.'s attention span, said: "One day a leaf flew in the window. He signed it."

Let's look at George W. in that light then: It's not that he really approved of what Dick Cheney, through Tony Snow, had to say about his father being responsible for what happened on 9/11; only that the boy had bigger leaves on his desk at the time.

Chapter 7

THE COULTERIZATION OF REPUBLICAN RHETORIC

"In many ways today's conservatives are party men and women not unlike those we saw in totalitarian countries, people who spout the line and slay the enemy without a thought as to the principles involved. Yes, they hate the Left. But only because the Left is the 'other'...They sometimes invoke the names of thinkers such as F. A. Hayek and Ludwig von Mises. But their real heroes are talk radio blabsters, television entertainers, and sexpot quipsters."

—LLEWELLYN H. ROCKWELL, JR., IN THE
AMERICAN CONSERVATIVE, AUGUST 2006

AMONG THE CRIMES AND misdemeanors I have to answer to a higher father for in the afterlife— aside from having voted for the Bush-Cheney ticket in the year 2000—is having served as Spiro Agnew's press secretary during the first Nixon administration.

Understand, I said *answer*, not apologize for—at least not in Agnew's case. Though I can't condone his having taken money in envelopes—a hangover from his days as governor of Maryland—I now see that malefaction in terms of his having been born thirty years too soon. Had the fallen vice president arrived in the nation's capital in 1999, rather than 1969, he might have forsworn chump change in envelopes by merely joining the ranks of those U.S. senators and congressmen who today lawfully supplement their federal incomes by arranging to get their wives and offspring hired by corporate lobbying firms at six- and seven-figure salaries per annum.

But I digress. Dennis Hastert's money-churning K Street Project and similar refinements in the art of political influence peddling will be duly addressed. But for now, let's stay with the story of Spiro Agnew's five-year rise and fall as Richard Nixon's controversial, media-bashing vice president.

It was Agnew's unprecedented criticism of what he labeled "the sensation-seeking national press" that first brought me to his staff in the summer of 1970. Unprecedented because, though Washington and New York–bred correspondents and commentators had been criticized by public officials before, not until Nixon's vice president came along had anyone at that level of government dared do it publicly. The political rule at the time was "You can't fight the press, they always get the last word."

For the record, the Nixon-Agnew administration wasn't the first to flout that rule. Early in the Kennedy administration, the president, displeased with coverage of the White House by a major New York daily, publicly cancelled his subscription to the *New York Herald Tribune*. That, however, was more a slap on the wrist than a full-spirited attack. Later in the 1960s, a Democratic congressional committee attacked a CBS documentary hosted by Edward R. Murrow (*Hunger in America*) for misrepresenting a prematurely born infant as a baby dying of malnutrition. And following the chaotic Democratic national convention of 1968, Chicago mayor Richard Daley and Democrats on the House Commerce Committee blasted all three television networks for their coverage of antiwar street demonstrations in Lincoln Park.

But Agnew's criticism of the national media came as a sustained, comprehensive assault, seamlessly attached to his sharply edged attacks on members of the Democratic opposition; to the extent that the most famous (or, depending on your perspective, infamous) Agnevian phrase passed down through the years—"nattering nabobs of negativism"—while actually directed at a quartet of Democratic senators, is generally thought to refer to journalists.

Though it wasn't, the vice president's speeches during that period contained other pungent, though non-alliterative, phrases aimed at various administration critics (re college campus demonstrators: "an elite corps of impudent snobs who characterize themselves as intellectuals"), with the news media high on the target list.

Flashback, Des Moines, Iowa, November 13, 1969: This was the speech that made Spiro Agnew both a conservative hero and one of the most controversial vice presidents in American history. In a nationally televised address before Midwest Republicans, he condemned the growing power of major news organizations answerable, he charged, to no one but themselves. ("Nowhere in our system are there fewer checks on vast power... [I]t represents a concentration of power over American public opinion unknown in history.")

For those of the post–Vietnam/Watergate era who might find those words hyperbolic, let's look back at the media environment of that period: They were years when a speaker referring to "the mainstream media" would get only a puzzled look from his audience. What other kind of media was there?

As President Lyndon Johnson remarked (though not in public speeches), there were only "two wire services (AP and UPI), two newspapers (the New York Times and Washington Post), two magazines (Time and Newsweek), and three networks (CBS, NBC, and ABC) that accounted for 90 percent" of what the American people knew of the world around them.

It was a monopoly with a Left-leaning news slant, argued Agnew. In a follow-up speech on the media, delivered in Montgomery, Alabama, on November 20, 1969, he called for "a broader spectrum of national opinion" among "commentators of the network news" and on the editorial pages of the New York Times and Washington Post: "Men who can articulate other points of view should be brought forward."

This, as a matter of journalistic history, is exactly what happened in the aftermath of Agnew's two speeches. The networks in the early 1970s began featuring conservative commentators

(George Will on ABC, James J. Kilpatrick on CBS), and major dailies across the country found space for Op-Ed pages featuring points-of-view other than those of the editors. Conservative columnists like William Safire and Will, whose views would have gone unpublished a decade earlier, were, as Agnew had urged, "brought forward" by the Times and the Post.

Still, what memories there are of Spiro Agnew's four controversial years as vice president relate to his forced resignation from office and reputation for employing what in those days passed for polarizing, divisive rhetoric (e.g., "nattering nabobs," "impudent snobs," "self-appointed elitists," etc.).

Polarizing? By today's standard of vice presidential rhetoric, the man would be considered—to borrow one of his own favorite terms—a "pusillanimous pussy-footer."

***

MSNBC News Services, November 17, 2005: Cheney Calls War Critics "Opportunists"

Washington—In the sharpest White House attack yet on critics of the Iraq war, Vice President Dick Cheney said on Wednesday that accusations the Bush administration manipulated intelligence to justify the war were a "dishonest and reprehensible" political ploy. Cheney called Democrats "opportunists" who were peddling "cynical and pernicious falsehoods to gain political advantage while U.S. soldiers died in Iraq."

Dishonest and reprehensible opportunists who play politics while U.S. soldiers are dying.

And that, as former Georgia Senator Max Cleland could testify if the Bush-Cheney White House were ever brought to the bar for "polarizing" politics, was just a love tap. Though dozens of Democratic (and out-of-goose-step Republican) candidates across the country have been tarred by accusations of being "soft on terrorism" after crossing the administration on war policy, Cleland stands out as the prize trophy on the White House wall of bagged political enemies.

But if this vice president is his administration's lead headhunter in its domestic war on criticism, he does not, as did Spiro Agnew, go after his game as a lone rifle. By the time Max Cleland had wrapped up his campaign for reelection, he'd been worked over by one of Karl Rove's prime political hit men, Ralph Reed, morphed by TV admen into Saddam Hussein and Osama bin Laden, and called—by the administration's shrillest defender among Bush-Cheney talk radio blabsters—a bemedaled imposter who had actually lost both legs and an arm in Vietnam by, she acidly claimed, *"being run over by a truck while in a drunken stupor outside an Army PX."*

Meet Ann Coulter, Intelligent Design's gift to late-night comedians who run out of Bush, Cheney, and Clinton material. And, ironically, to the very Liberals she loves to hate.

What better gift to the polemical Left than a shrill, ball-busting caricature of your conservative opposition? A "sexpot quipster," as Lew Rockwell aptly calls her, who biliously writes that the way to deal with hostile Muslim populations is to "invade their countries, kill their leaders, and convert them to Christianity."

Is she serious or just trying to sell books? Makes no difference. Serious or not, her shrieking diatribes against Liberals, Democrats, "rag heads," "wetbacks," "Jersey broads" (applied to anti-Bush widows of 9/11 victims)— anyone who so much as winces when the Wartime Leader's name comes up—merely reflects, in its crudest form, the White House-RNC party line.

Indeed, not merely reflects but *is* the White House party line. I've seen other administrations try to cultivate the news media with varying success, but under Karl Rove's direction, the Bush-Cheney White House has put together a stable of columnists and commentators who, in return for special treatment, operate as a virtual arm of Tony Snow's press office (Snow himself having once been part of the stable).[1]

Coulter's viperous assault on Cleland, for example—a paraplegic recipient of the Silver Star for bravery under fire—fit perfectly into Rove's take-no-prisoners game plan for Republican candidates in 2002: attack all Democratic candidates as being "soft" on homeland security, the

---

[1] Special treatment coming in the form of invitations to White House socials and extraordinary access to administration higher-ups, including the President and Vice President, along with early warning tips on breaking news. Among Rove's favorite columnists: Fred Barnes of the *Weekly Standard*, David Brooks of the *New York Times* and the *Washington Post*'s Charles Krauthammer. In a separate category, needless to say, were those purportedly "independent" opinion makers like columnist/commentator Armstrong Williams, revealed as having been paid through a PR conduit for articles spouting the White House line on controversial issues.

Patriot Act, and Justice Department surveillance programs put into place after 9/11.

The game plan worked beyond expectations in 2002, not only by defeating Cleland in Georgia but also in reversing the usual pattern of White House party losses in mid-term elections. Predictably, that success made the Rove strategy of tying 9/11 and the war in Iraq into one neat demagogic package *de rigueur* for GOP candidates in all future elections.

"Soft on terrorism" was a charge leveled at John Kerry in 2004 (along with the accusation that the Democratic presidential candidate, like Cleland, was a bemedaled imposter). By 2006, Rove's mailed hand obvious, the rhetorical gambit had been fine-tuned to include, for historical weight, the charge that those who didn't fall into line with the administration's "stay the course" war plans were, in Donald Rumsfeld's alarmist words, short-sighted "appeasers" of "Islamo-fascism," comparable to Britain's umbrella-carrying Neville Chamberlain in 1938. (The threadbare Munich analogy again, revived from the Vietnam War era.)

It would be twisting history, a la Rumsfeld, to imply that this administration is the first to use dying American soldiers as a propaganda bludgeon against its critics. But no administration since the 20th-century advent of mass communications has ever had the luxury, as does the Bush-Cheney White House, of wielding its bludgeon with a media of its own.

Oh, what Richard Nixon wouldn't have given for talk radio and Fox News to have been around in the 1970s. Impeachment? By the time Rush Limbaugh and Bill O'Reilly were finished with Sam Irvin and Peter Rodino, the Watergate committee chairmen would have been lucky to have their spaniels greet them at the door when they arrived home after a hard day's hearings. I can hear it now...

> *Rush Limbaugh*: Here we go again, people. Just off the wire, this year's poster boy for the North Carolina chapter of the Ho Chi Minh Fan Club— you remember Cornpone Sam Irvin? "Ah'm justa simple country lawyer..." He'll get no argument here—he's as simple as they come. And now Simple Sam, according to a press flyer from his Senate Watergate Committee, wants the president to turn all those White House tapes over so that he and his super-Lib cronies on the Hill can play partisan kick-ball with 'em. *All* the tapes, people, including the top-secret talks, war plans America's enemies in Moscow and Hanoi would just love to hear...

Or for those who like their Righteous bile served in prime time...

> *Bill O'Reilly*: So you'll know, after last night's interview with Gordon Liddy, one of the few reliable sources left in the nation's capital these days, we invited Peter Rodino, chairman of the House committee investigating the alleged Watergate break-in,

to come on the show, no-strings, no time limit, to answer the charge that in his first race for Congress he took a five-hundred-dollar donation from one Angelo Marcantonio who, it turns out, was a blood cousin of the old Left-wing congressman Vito Marcantonio, best remembered for being on the FBI's top ten list of communist sympathizers...

Not to forget the bloggers who'd have set the record straight on Watergate (a CIA-KGB conspiracy) as well as the under-the-table payoffs to syndicated columnists to hawk the Nixon party line (a Bush-Cheney innovation Tricky Dick would have loved).

But no such luck, people. All Nixon had back then was what we now call the "mainstream media" (MSM). What's more, things would stay that way until the Reagan '80s, when, first, the Federal Communications Commission repealed the Fairness Doctrine and, next, an immigrant billionaire Aussie with a Rightist bent, one Rupert Murdoch, moved in to change the face and tone of cable news. Finally, it seemed, conservatives had a way to get their message through to a mass audience. But for the life of me, I don't think the message sent, despite its Rightward slant, was quite what Spiro Agnew and conservatives of that era had in mind.

✱ ✱ ✱

The conservative message from the 1950s to the Reagan era was best reflected in the pages of William F. Buckley's *National Review* and in the books and columns written by

Buckley, James J. Kilpatrick, William Safire, and George Will. These and other lesser-known conservative writers offered readers a thoughtful, if provocative, mix of Right-wing ideology and political analysis that went beyond mere anti-Liberal polemics. Then came the Limbaugh-Fox Revolution and, as Agnew said of the "sensation-seeking" media of his own day, a journalistic Gresham's Law set in—the bad driving out the good.

The Limbaugh-Fox Revolution

On those rare occasions when he thought to share credit for the Republican takeover of the House of Representatives in 1994, Newt Gingrich spoke glowingly of the contribution Rush Limbaugh and talk radio had made in bringing about "the Gingrich Revolution."

And well he should have. As the undisputed king of the talk radio blabsters, Limbaugh himself led a revolution (or more accurately, shared leadership with Fox News president Roger Ailes) in the way Manichean media changed the nation's political culture.[2]

Gingrich spoke of the process as "the new media," as opposed to the old media that Republicans since the 1950s

---

[2] Manichean media: News and opinion reportage/commentary best described by the book title chosen by Clintonite talk-blabsters James Carville and Paul Begala, *We're Right, They're Wrong*. It's not as if the activist Right has a monopoly on the just-kill-the-bastards view of political discourse (as MoveOn.org and the weird world of Radical Left bloggers demonstrate daily). Only that the Right has proven more adept at it, commercially and otherwise.

felt were stacked against their interests. But with Limbaugh leading the way, a veritable army of Clinton-bashing, Bush-defending talk show hosts came into their own in the 1990s, the hard-line Right's answer to the MSM.

There was irony in that. Using radio to counter perceived conservative bias in the print media of the day was the technique hit upon in the 1930s by the architect of modern Liberalism, Franklin Roosevelt. It was through his weekly "Fireside Chats" that FDR got through to the masses, spouting his line and slaying his enemies—the "economic royalists" he said were bent on blocking his New Deal programs.

Twenty years later, with the advent of television, radio was supposedly dead as a major political medium. But with the elimination of the Fairness Doctrine, partisan political banter with no holds barred was loosed upon the land, this time around as a Republican weapon to smite FDR's political heirs.

I leave it to focus-group gurus to do the research on why the most outrageously successful of today's talkshow blabsters, Limbaugh, O'Reilly, Sean Hannity, and Hugh Hewitt are on the Right. For my part, I see Limbaugh's success, along with that of his talk radio imitators, as a matter of framing political discourse in blue-collar populist terms—news and commentary, as packaged by World Wrestling Entertainment.

(Survey fact: Though a vast majority of Limbaugh's listeners describe themselves as conservative, his daily radio blab fest also attracts a sizeable audience of Liberals who tune in just to get their blood boiling.)

I don't know Limbaugh, but I do know Roger Ailes, having watched him at work during George H. W.'s successful 1988 presidential campaign. By 1992, Roger had left the field of campaign communications, in transit to taking on the challenge of putting together an international cable news network for Rupert Murdoch; a setback for George, I thought at the time, as he could have used Ailes's keen strategic mind and technical skills to help close the five-point edge Bill Clinton held throughout the race.

Whether the gap could have been narrowed, I can't say. What I do know is that Ailes' genius for political combat-by-camera was the single most important element in George's overcoming the spurious "wimp" charge the Democrats and mainstream media had worked overtime to saddle him with during the campaign (Ann Richards at the convention, *Newsweek* with a tricked-up cover).

It all began when Dan Rather (remember him?) invited Vice President Bush to the CBS newsroom for a live interview, supposedly a supplement to a short film clip reviewing Bush's career. A similar interview and film clip covering Michael Dukakis proved harmless enough, Rather playing it straight in laying out the Democratic candidate's career as governor of Massachusetts. Dan had a different scenario in mind for Bush, however. Ailes, who was prepping the vice president for the session, got wind of the CBS anchor's plan to use the interview not to cover Bush's long career in politics—congressman, ambassador, CIA director, vice president—but to blindside him on Iran-Contra, the Oliver North–planned guns-for-funds scandal that had rocked the second Reagan administration.

A lesser political strategist would have advised his candidate to pull the plug on the session, allowing Rather to gaze sincerely into the camera, look at an empty chair, and tell his audience that though he'd invited Bush to be interviewed, the vice president, unlike Governor Dukakis, had for some reason declined (sigh, possibly a feigned look of puzzlement). Ailes, however, had Rather's number: Not only would Bush proceed with the interview, he'd go into it primed to trap his would-be trapper.

Rather was notorious as a TV prima donna and had stalked out of a studio in a fit of pique on one memorable occasion, leaving an eight-minute program gap that darkened TV screens for CBS viewers. So informed by Ailes, Bush waited for his inquisitor to bear down on Iran-Contra, then turned the tables on Rather by saying it was as wrong to focus on that one issue "as it would be if we judged *your* entire career by that eight minutes you walked out of that studio in Miami and let the screen go black."

Unglued, Rather stumbled through the rest of the session, then later complained that Bush, by bringing up the Miami incident, had unfairly "sandbagged" him. (In fact, as the Bush campaign was later advised by CBS insiders, Rather had spent the better part of an afternoon rehearsing ways to sandbag Bush, even staging a mock interview, his show's producer filling in as the vice president.)

Ailes demonstrated that same combination of creativity and combativeness in his launch of Rupert Murdoch's Fox News network. Unlike CNN, the cable news pioneer, Fox would have a sharp political edge, in line with its owner's London tabloid background. Fox would not only be a throwback, albeit in electronic form, to the partisan American journals of the 19th and early 20th centuries, but would also reflect the party line of Murdoch's Neo-Con opinion magazine, the *Weekly Standard*.

That in mind, Murdoch, himself a throwback to the early 20th-century days when media moguls were strong-willed individualists—Hearst, McCormick, Pulitzer—had picked the right man to build his global news network: Roger Ailes was not only a skilled television producer but also a master of the universe in delivering the Right-wing political message to a mass audience.

Under Ailes' leadership, Fox News would emerge in a relatively short time as the number one cable news service in the world and, with the coming of a Republican administration in Washington, an influential, White House-favored news-gathering agency in the nation's capital.

When Donald Rumsfeld felt the urge to unload on his Democratic and mainstream press critics, his press office had only to call Sean Hannity and set up a softball chat-fest, prime-time; when Dick Cheney felt the need to talk publicly about his embarrassing hunting accident in Texas, he called on Brit Hume, the respected ABC correspondent Ailes hired to run Fox's Washington bureau, to conduct the interview; and when Scott McClellan stepped down as the Bush White House press secretary in the summer of 2006, who better to replace him than a personable journalist/commentator who had honed his skills as a program anchor for, who else, Fox News?

That, of course, would be Tony Snow, doing officially, on the White House payroll, the same job he'd been doing unofficially all these years on Rupert Murdoch's payroll: protecting Dubya's backside from the caviling herd Richard Nixon used to call "the goddamn Liberal press."

* * *

"I wonder if they're more interested in protecting the terrorists than protecting the American people."

—HOUSE REPUBLICAN LEADER JOHN BOEHNER, TAKING ON DEMOCRATIC CRITICS OF THE WHITE HOUSE WAR ON TERROR, SEPTEMBER 12, 2006

It's contagious, you see. Check John Boehner's early record as an Ohio congressman to learn that he'd never be one to play knee-in-the-groin politics. But when you step into Tom DeLay's shoes as House majority leader, which Boehner did in early 2006, you either do things Tom's way or the hang-'em-high crowd you're leading won't be happy; nor will the Republican White House that started it all four years earlier.

You're Either For Us or Against Us. It seemed an apt rhetorical flourish when George W., in his State of the Union following 9/11, framed the war on terror in those Biblical terms. What we didn't know at the time was that the "us" he referred to meant simply him, Dick Cheney, and Donald Rumsfeld. Or that the events of 9/11, which had unified the country in a way Americans hadn't known since the bombing of Pearl Harbor, would bring on the worst era of Us-versus-Them partisanship in half a century, Dubya's politically aggressive White House setting the tone.

Democrats, now on the receiving end of a White House–inspired campaign of fear and division, may be heard to complain, but in this case—much as Bush, Cheney, and the Rummy have pushed that envelope—there's a precedent, one I remember all too well.

Flashback once more, this time to the fall of 1964 when Lyndon Johnson, even with a two-digit lead in the polls, directed his White House attack mandarin, Bill Moyers, to work over his opponent, Barry Goldwater, with a series of negative campaign spots.

Goldwater, whom I never knew to mention either Johnson's or Moyers' name without an expletive, described in his autobiography the way dirty-trick politics, as practiced by a Texas White House, played out back then...

From Goldwater, by Barry M. Goldwater and Jack Casserly (1988):

> *Moyers ordered two "bomb" commercials from the New York advertising firm of Doyle Dane Bernbach. He oversaw and approved their production. The first was a one-minute film that appeared during prime time on NBC. It showed a little girl in a sunny field of daisies. She begins plucking petals from a daisy. As she plucks the flower, a male voice in the background starts a countdown...ten...nine...eight...becoming constantly stronger. The screen suddenly explodes, and the*

child disappears in a mushroom cloud. The voice concludes by urging voters to elect President Johnson, saying, "These are the stakes: To make a world in which all of God's children can live, or go into the dark. We must either love each other or we must die. Vote for President Johnson on November third. The stakes are too high for you to stay home." There was no doubt as to the meaning: Barry Goldwater would blow up the world if he became President of the United States.

Nor was that the last advertising bomb the White House would drop in its campaign-of-fear against LBJ's Republican opponent in 1964. One week later, a second Doyle Dane Bernbach TV spot appeared on network television, this one featuring an ice cream cone...

A soft, motherly voice explained in the background that radioactive fallout had killed many children. A treaty had been signed to prevent such destruction. The gloomy voice said a man—Barry Goldwater—had voted against the Nuclear Test Ban Treaty. A Geiger counter rose to a crescendo as a male voice concluded: "Vote for Lyndon Johnson on November third...the stakes are too high to stay at home."

That commercial, as Goldwater argued to the Fair Campaign Practices Committee, "completely misrepresented my position, which called for treaty guarantees and other safeguards for the United States." The FCPC agreed and told the Democratic National Committee to drop the ads. They were dropped, but the damage to Goldwater and his campaign couldn't be undone.

"Those bomb commercials," Barry would recall, "were the start of dirty political ads on television. Moyers and the New York firm will long be remembered for helping to launch this ugly development in our political history."

Or at least he hoped they would, but to paraphrase one of Barry's own heroes, Winston Churchill, it all depends on who's writing the history: Four decades later, Moyers, one of those untouched Teflon personalities in mainstream media circles, is thought of as a furrow-browed producer of documentaries for public broadcasting rather than Lyndon Johnson's White House hatchet man.

Not that all the "dirty" political attacks on Barry Goldwater in 1964 came from the White House. There were also biased editors and reporters, both print and electronic, who covered the campaign in a way that led Barry to comment, post-election, that "If all I knew about that fella Goldwater was what I read in the papers, I wouldn't have voted for the sonofabitch myself."

The network news legend David Brinkley, ever candid, once said that the idea of a political reporter being without bias is absurd. Bias goes with being human, Brinkley explained, and the best a newsman can do is recognize his own biases and try to curb them.

In Goldwater's case, unfortunately, the Brinkley Rule was given the spike by a great many editors and reporters. Never—at least not in the modern era—has a presidential candidate, Republican or Democrat, been so maligned in terms of both who he was and what he stood for. It's true,

Barry's war record wasn't distorted by either the White House or its closeted friends in the media, but other than that, little of his reputation went through the campaign unscathed.

Media Dirty Tricks?

Even Goldwater's sanity was challenged, in a "psychological study" published by *Fact* magazine that began with the question "Do you think that Barry Goldwater is psychologically fit to serve as president of the United States?" A poll of two thousand unnamed psychiatrists, give or take a registered Democrat, came forward with a "No" answer, but though the "poll" was ridiculed by the American Psychiatric Association, the image of Goldwater as an unstable personality again came through. (After the campaign, a libel suit filed by Goldwater won a financial judgment that put the magazine out of business.)

For all of its sixty-four pages, however, the *Fact* study did minimal harm compared to that of a single sentence appearing in the *New York Times* beneath the byline of *Times* publisher C. L. Sulzberger: "The possibility exists," wrote Sulzberger, "that should [Goldwater] enter the White House, there might not be a day after tomorrow."

Wait, there's worse: A CBS report from the network's overseas correspondent, Daniel Schorr, "reliably" had it that following the Republican convention Goldwater would travel to Berchtesgaden, Bavaria, Hitler's old "Eagle's Nest," to address a neo-Nazi group!

Cliché time: What goes around, comes around, those of us who worked with Goldwater are tempted to say whenever a Limbaugh or Coulter drops a dirty bomb on one of LBJ's Democratic heirs.

But then, second thoughts: Is that why we worked all those years to put a conservative Republican in the White House? To bring back the political ethics of Lyndon Johnson and Bill Moyers?

Chapter 8

THEIR EYES HAVE SEEN THE GLORY (THE THEO-CON AGENDA)

"I think that the White House understands that the largest constituency in the Republican party on election day are people who are regularly in church on Sunday and then are in the voting booth on Tuesday... [W]e are the heart of the party."

—GARY BAUER, PRESIDENT, AMERICAN VALUES

U NFORTUNATELY, GARY BAUER IS right. Not only have he and his fellow Theo-Cons taken over the party of Lincoln nationally, but state by state as well. Consider only the disastrous—no, farcical is a better word —Republican effort in 2004 to win a U.S. Senate seat in Lincoln's own state.

Jim Ryan, the GOP nominee for the Senate seat vacated by Peter Fitzgerald, had to withdraw from the race after a highly publicized domestic scandal. Over a dozen possible replacements came forward—all Illinoisans—but the party's state Central Committee had someone else in mind. The fact that he wasn't an Illinois resident, that his only knowledge of the state came from passing through O'Hare Airport en route to speaking engagements, made no difference. Alan Keyes fit the Theo-Con-dominated Central Committee's idea of what the party of Lincoln should stand for in a society fallen on heathen Liberal ways.

Keyes, whose political experience at the time consisted of two embarrassing runs for the Republican presidential nomination and the same number for the U.S. Senate (in his home state of Maryland) is an African American whose reputation was based on hellfire-and-damnation speeches before moral conservative audiences enraptured by a black firebrand spouting words they loved to hear (e.g., "What distinguishes the terrorist from the ordinary warrior is that the terrorist will consciously target human life. What is done in the course of abortion? Someone consciously targets innocent human life.")

Red-meat oratory for the "pro-life" audience: How it would register with Illinois voters in general was questioned by old-line Illinois Republicans—the pre-takeover kind whose conservatism was defined by party leaders such as Everett Dirksen and Bob Michels. But the Central Committee had only to talk to Keyes once to know they had the God-sent candidate to face off against the Democrats' Barack Obama.

As Keyes himself described his appeal in a self-promotional flyer, he had "unashamedly and consistently raised the standard of unalienable rights—and Biblical truth—in defense of the unborn. He confronts the culture of death with compelling and inspiring reasons why abortion must be banned from our land."

So much for the moderate side of Alan Keyes' appeal to Illinois voters in his 2004 Senate race. Though without benefit of any of Karl Rove's political hit men, Keyes on his own managed to come up with an attack strategy that included calling his opponent "a hard-line, academic Marxist-socialist" as well as a "wicked" Democrat who "had been identified by the Catholic church as objectively evil."

Catholics who would vote for Barack Obama, continued Keyes, "make themselves part of that evil, just like the folks in Germany who voted for the party that eventually led to the Holocaust." And more: "Christ would not vote for Barack Obama," Keyes charged in the final days of the campaign, "because Barack Obama has voted to behave in a way that is inconceivable for Christ to behave." What the voters of Illinois were being offered by their state Republican party, in other words, was a candidate for the U.S. Senate not only in touch with Jesus—there are plenty of those, beginning with the True Believer in the Oval Office—but one in whom Jesus confides his voting preferences. It was over-the-line campaign rhetoric, yet there were no words of reproof, not even an eyebrow raised by members of the Illinois Republican party's Central Committee. This, after all, is what they'd brought their voluble Maryland import to town for—to spread the gospel and preach the agenda, win or lose. And lose Keyes did, his "Marxist-socialist" opponent receiving 70 percent of the vote to Keyes's 27 percent.

A lesson learned? Not at all. Political messianics, whether working out of the Oval Office in Washington or the Republican Central Committee in Springfield, have no lessons to learn, other than those delivered by Divine revelation. Alan Keyes would simply return to Maryland, a 21st-century Harold Stassen waiting for God's call to the next campaign, while Gary Bauer's Illinois champions of American values would blame their defeat on the usual suspects: (1) distortions by the Liberal media, (2) betrayals by non-church-going Republicans who weren't "in the voting booth on Tuesday," and (3) the evil machinations of the Cook County Democratic machine, its operatives behaving in a way that would be inconceivable for Christ, were he a vote tabulator, to behave.

In short, though the Illinois Theo-Con candidate might have lost the election, for the True Believers of the Religious Right it was only because his message hadn't gone through unfiltered. As for the message itself, their confidence in the agenda and its ultimate triumph remained unshaken. Like the radical cadres of the Jacobin Left who took over the Democratic party, state by state, in the McGovernite '70s, the Theo-Cons regard rejection at the polls, in the Congress, or in the courts, as mere vindication of their view that the American people are being misled by an evil conspiracy of power brokers in Washington and New York. Each defeat fuels their determination to press on with their mission, advance their agenda.

And what, beyond the overheated rhetoric of an Alan Keyes, is the Theocratic-Conservative agenda for 21st-century America? It begins, of course, with the reversal of *Roe v. Wade* by the Roberts-led Supreme Court, a virtual certainty should another vacancy occur during the Bush-43 presidency. Or perhaps beyond the Bush-43 presidency, given the uncertain trumpet being sounded by leading Democrats as they edge their way toward November 2008.

Front-Page Headline, New York Times, January 24, 2005: "Clinton Seeking Shared Ground Over Abortion"

Beneath the headline, a story covering a Hillary Clinton speech on the anniversary of *Roe v. Wade* in which the senator, in the words of one supporter, "updated" her message on abortion in the hope of "repositioning her party" on the issue.

Seeking Shared Ground

If the people Clinton hope to win over to a "shared" position on abortion are Gary Bauer, Alan Keyes, or Tony Perkins of the Family Research Council, she approaches the issue with, to put it kindly, uncharacteristic naïveté. When you open a dialogue on abortion with these or any other "pro-life" spokesman and the first words out of his mouth are "Abortion is murder," what's your response, Hillary? "Could we agree on, say, first-degree manslaughter?"

The issue, in a word seldom heard in American politics for a century and a half, is intractable, and the conflict between the opposing constituencies—"pro-life" and "pro-choice"—as irrepressible in the years ahead as that between North and South in the 1860s.[1]

Should *Roe v. Wade* be reversed, even in part, the battleground will simply shift to the grassroots, where the holy warriors of Theo-Con persuasion and women's rights groups will carry on their missions in fifty state legislatures, with the shrieking rhetoric that Illinois Republicans encouraged in the Keyes campaign more the norm than the exception.

Indeed, warming up for that day, consider only the title of a 2006 book written by *National Review* senior editor Ramesh Ponnuru: *The Party of Death: The Democrats, the Media, the Courts, and the Disregard for Human Life.* (Come on, Ramesh, tell us what you *really* think about Democrats.)

By anything other than Alan Keyes' standards, that's over the top. But attention must be paid a Princeton scholar (summa cum laude in history) who, having given serious thought to the way in which the death-dealers operate, argues "that the same process by which the party of death has made such deep inroads into American society can now be used in reverse: Pro-lifers must strive harder than ever to restrict abortion and ultimately to end it altogether, for the more we reject abortion, the more we might come to reject other choices for death."[2]

Read, at one end of Ponnuru's rejection syndrome, Terri Schiavo, and at the other end, stem cell research, each

---

[1] The same could be said of all issues on the Theo-Con agenda: same-sex liaisons, gays in the military, stem-cell research. But nothing comes close to abortion as a defining issue in what members of the Religious Right see as a war for the national soul.

reflecting the second item on the Theo-Con agenda, right-to-life issues.

Once, in the not-too-distant past, the term "pro-life" was taken to mean hard-line opposition to abortion and no more. Euthanasia, for example, had always been condemned by Gary Bauer's church-going regulars, but as an electric issue that could motivate the evangelical base, the Dr. Kevorkian case had minimal ogre value outside Michigan. That would change, however, and "pro-life" would take on a new, expanded meaning, with the Republican capture of Congress in the mid-'90s and the White House in 2001.

One of the first base-rousing issues to reach George W.'s desk, in fact, came with his decision regarding federal involvement in stem cell research. It was important enough, in Karl Rove's eyes, to warrant a prime-time televised address from the Crawford, Texas, ranch, a speech in which the president seemingly bobbed-and-weaved his way around the issue, pro and con. The government would fund, he announced, "some sixty self-sustaining lines of embryos already in existence, juxtaposing the need to protect life *in all its phases* with the prospect of saving and improving life in all its stages" (emphasis added).

---

[2] Ponnuru shows no similar rejection of "other choices of death" when the question of the Bush-Cheney war in Iraq comes up. A dogmatic Neo-Con as well as fanatic Theo-Con, he excoriated Father Andrew Greeley following 9/11 when Greeley took issue with "the national cry for revenge" and the killing of innocent civilians in wartime. Nonsense, responded Ponnuru, making the case for his own culture of death: War, he wrote, means killing and if innocent civilians suffer collateral damage, tough luck. (But if, in the bombing we were to hit an in vitro clinic in Baghdad, what then, Ramesh? Blame it on a Democratic bombardier?)

I emphasize the phrase now, though I confess its significance passed me by at the time it was uttered, as did two earlier lines in the speech: "Research on embryonic stem cells raises profound ethical questions, because extracting the stem cell destroys the embryo, and thus destroys its potential for life. Like a snowflake, each of these embryos is unique, with the unique genetic potential of an individual human being."

There it was, plain as day for those of us who had voted for George W. Bush and were cynical enough to think that all his self-centered blather about being in personal touch with the Lord was, in Wendell Willkie's famous phrase, "mere campaign oratory." (True, Dubya went to church on Sunday, quoted the Bible, joined hands in singing gospel, kept his marriage vows, and didn't drink. But that proved nothing in terms of his religious sincerity. With the exception of the last two items, the same could be said of Bill Clinton.)

But the speech in the summer of 2001 was only a wake-up call for smart-ass cynics like me. Five years later, if there were still any around who thought Dubya was anything other than the Bible-quoting True Believer he claimed to be, all doubt was removed on a hot and humid August day in Washington...

Priorities

Though he'd promised to shrink the size of government, cut federal spending, reduce the deficit, and usher in a new era of public accountability, George W. Bush, after more than five years in office, had failed to lift a finger, much less veto a bill in order to check the power of a profligate, free-wheeling Congress dominated by his own party, until...

"In First Veto, Bush Blocks Stem Cell Bill"

—FRONT-PAGE HEADLINE, *NEW YORK TIMES*, JULY 19, 2006

And he'd do it with Hollywood flair, in a White House ceremony surrounded, according to the *Times* story, by happy children and their smiling parents. Dozens of kids, the president noted, who were born as a result of an embryo-adoption program.

"This bill," intoned Bush, explaining his veto, "would support the taking of innocent human life with inherent dignity and matchless value." Then, with a flourish, as he turned to the kids: "These boys and girls are not spare parts!"

No argument there, but I had to wonder, watching the staged ceremony on television, how supporters of the bill on Capitol Hill—including Republican leaders like Bill Frist, Orrin Hatch, and Arlen Specter—would take to their president's implication that they were not only morally insensitive to "taking innocent human life," but saw the animated boys and girls applauding Bush as mere "spare parts."

I wondered, but then realized, that as carapaced political veterans, they'd take it as part of the game, mere campaign oratory. One call from the White House to say, "The President and Laura will be happy to attend your fundraiser, senator," and all would be well on Capitol Hill; at least among Republicans.

But beyond that, operative lines from George W.'s previous stem cell speech came to mind. The lines, retrieved from White House speech files of August 2001, read:

"As the discoveries of modern science create tremendous hope, they also lay vast ethical minefields. As the genius of science extends the horizons of what we can do, we increasingly confront complex questions about what we should do. We have arrived at that brave new world that seemed so distant in 1932, when Aldous Huxley wrote about human beings created in test tubes in what he called a 'hatchery.'"

Aldous Huxley and *Brave New World*—I'd never considered the stem cell issue in those mechanistic terms, but since George W. himself raised the point, my question to the moralizing Decider in his Hollywood moment would have been, "At what point between using stem cells to alleviate human suffering and, given your veto, letting them go to waste, do we move into that ethical minefield you warn against?"

* * *

"Terry Schiavo was brought to us by God to elevate the visibility of what's going on in America."
—House Majority Leader Tom DeLay, spring, 2005

In Tom Delay's eyes, as we might have guessed, God isn't just a registered Republican but an activist who works up wedge issues to keep the party base engaged. Too bad for Terri Schiavo, but somebody had to take the fall in order to "elevate the visibility" of the Democrats' culture of death.

No event or pseudo-event since the rise of the Theo-Cons in the 1980s better exemplifies their contempt for traditional conservative values than the crass exploitation of the Terri Schiavo case by a Republican White House and congressional majority in the spring of 2005.

The Facts

A young Florida woman suffers severe brain damage and goes into what one court describes as "a persistent vegetative state." She's kept alive for the next fifteen years on a support system, until her feeding tube is removed at the request of her husband, who says his wife wouldn't have wanted to live in that condition. When the woman's parents sue to enjoin the removal of the feeding tube, a five-member state medical panel, after examining the evidence, concludes there is no hope for recovery. But backed by a fervid evangelical network, the parents, having exhausted all legal remedies in the state of Florida, take their case to Washington, asking Congress to order the federal courts to intervene.

Pause here to get our political and, more importantly, constitutional bearings: For point of reference, no Congress in history—not even the most liberal, loose-constructionist Congress of the New Deal or Great Society eras—ever considered ordering the federal courts to take jurisdiction over an individual case involving powers reserved to the states.

But this, nevertheless, is exactly what the divinely inspired "conservative" Republican Congress determined to do in March 2005. Led in the House by the sanctimonious likes of Dennis Hastert and his puppet-master Tom DeLay and in the Senate by the weak-spined Senate Majority Leader Bill Frist, both houses of Congress set aside all national business—homeland security, immigration reform, the federal budget—in order to enact "emergency" legislation directing the federal court of appeals in Atlanta to take jurisdiction over the Schiavo case.

Theocracy in action, fueled by the tabloid sensibilities of talk radio blabsters, the ratings chase of cable TV news, and, most of all, the fulminating political passion of True Believers like Gary Bauer. Consider for example, this excerpt from Bauer's open newsletter of March 24, 2005:

To: Friends and Supporters
From: Gary L. Bauer
President, American Values

An increasing number of people are asking why Terri Schiavo cannot be given crushed ice or a sip of water. The court order required that her feeding tube be removed—what the other side refers to as "pulling the plug," as if she were an appliance. But, police posted at the door block any attempt to give her water or nourishment by mouth. A whole family, including children, was arrested yesterday for attempting to give her a sip of water.

Harvard University lecturer William Anderson, writing today in the online edition of the *Weekly Standard*, brought this issue into sharp focus. He points out that her neurological damage may prevent her from swallowing and giving her water could raise the danger of developing "aspiration pneumonia." But we don't know that to be the case, so why not try? How can providing her with water or pureed food by mouth make things any worse? And on what moral or ethical grounds do we withhold these things from her?

Tomorrow, Christians will commemorate the Crucifixion of Christ. In the Gospel of Matthew, Chapter 25, verses 35 and 36, Jesus says, "For I was hungry and you gave me food, I was thirsty and you gave me drink, I was a stranger and you welcomed me." His disciples were puzzled and asked when had they done those things for him. Christ responds (verse 40), "Truly, I say to you, as you did it to one of the least of these my brethren, you did it for me."

Surely, Terri Schiavo, abandoned by her husband, sentenced to death by our courts, regularly compared to a "vegetable," qualifies as "the least of these." Will someone give her a drink?

Don't cringe. Bauer was one of the more *moderate* voices heard among the religious activists calling for action in the Save Terri movement. No one following Tom DeLay's political lead, after all—including DeLay himself—really expected the Devil's own federal court system to do anything but rule once again that it had no jurisdiction in the case.

No, the true voice of the movement, cutting through all the legalistic blather contained in the U.S. Constitution and the federal system, was that of the Right to Life militants in Florida who said *To hell with the courts* and called on Governor Jeb Bush to send in the National Guard to set things right; which is exactly what Tom the Exterminator, if he'd had his druthers, would have ordered, fixed bayonets at the ready.

* * *

Headline, *Washington Post*, August 3, 2005:
"Bush Remarks on 'Intelligent Design' Theory Fuel Debate"

President Bush invigorated proponents of teaching alternatives to evolution in public schools with remarks saying that schoolchildren should be taught about "intelligent design," a view of creation that challenges established scientific thinking and promotes the idea that an unseen force is behind the development of humanity.

Bush told Texas newspaper editors at the White House on Monday that he believes that intelligent design should be taught as competing theories. "Both sides should be properly taught," Bush said, "so people can understand what the debate is all about."

Progress

If William Jennings Bryan had been elected president in either 1896 or 1900, Americans would have had a man in the White House who didn't believe in Darwin's theory of evolution; a century later, we have a man in the White House who says he can take Darwin or leave him. So much for the value of a Yale-Harvard education.

Who would have thought that eight decades after the 1925 Scopes Trial in Dayton, Tennessee, Bryan's cantankerous "Don't call me a monkey," argument against Darwin's theory of evolution would return (albeit in novel form) to the national debate on what our children should or shouldn't be taught in school?

Intelligent Design

Is it really an alternative to Darwin? The Vatican itself having said there's nothing in Darwin's theory incompatible with the theology of Creation, what's all the fuss about? Simply this: The pseudo-scientific Holy Rollers promoting Intelligent Design want it that way. What we have here are the theological heirs of the wool hats who tried John Scopes, reshaping the argument against Darwin to put themselves on the politically correct side of academic freedom and open-mindedness. But make no mistake, the real goal is not simply to counter Darwin but to put the stamp of theologically correct thinking on all aspects of American education.

Not that, if the Holy Rollers have their way, Galileo's theory of how the solar system operates won't be taught in our public schools. It will; along, of course, with the opinion of the ecclesiastical court that tried him. After all, as our president so brilliantly put it, "Both sides should be properly taught, so people can understand what the debate is all about."

Chapter 9

THE K STREET CAPER

"Those who have been in government should not be forbidden from helping people deal with government, which is what I see myself doing. I'm earning significant multiples of what I've ever earned before."

—John Ashcroft on being the first former Attorney General in

U.S. history to register as a lobbyist, March 2006

"I want all their money!!!! Weez gonna be rich!!!"

—Email from Michael Scanlon, former Tom DeLay staff member,

to Jack Abramoff, re their lobbying rip-off

of the Tigua and Coushatta Indian tribes

WHEN JOHN ASHCROFT LOST his U.S. Senate seat to a corpse back in 2000, I passed on some gratuitous advice to one of his friends in Washington. I didn't know Ashcroft personally, though we'd met at a dinner party in Georgetown years before, when his name was being floated as a possible chairman for the Republican National Committee.

What Ashcroft had going for him, I was told, were his strong ties to James Dobson's Focus on the Family, the evangelical powerhouse that had replaced both Pat Robertson's Christian Coalition and Jerry Falwell's Moral Majority as the political spearhead of the Religious Right in the 1990s. Though Ashcroft wouldn't get the job, it was only because his Senate duties precluded his serving full time.

But back to a corpse winning a Senate seat in Missouri, a case of the Show-Me State exceeding its neighbor Illinois, where in Cook County people in cemeteries have been said to vote but never, as far as we know, been elected to office.

What happened in Missouri in the fall of 2000 was that Mel Carnahan, the popular governor nominated by the state Democratic party to challenge Ashcroft in his bid for reelection, was killed in a plane crash three weeks before the election, too late to remove his name from the ballot. That left the party chiefs with the choice of conceding the election to Ashcroft or, thinking outside-the-box—literally—asking voters to show their respect for Mel's memory by electing him posthumously (The slogan: "We're Still with Mel"). The incoming governor, a Democrat, would then appoint Mel's widow to fill the vacancy.

If ever there were an anybody-but vote, this would be it. What the election came down to was Missourians going to the polls to either endorse or repudiate the Ashcroft record. Repudiate they did, and while the rest of the country laughed at Ashcroft's expense, Missouri Democrats put plans in motion to send Jean Carnahan to Washington to represent the state until a special election could be held in the year 2002.

As I say, I didn't know John Ashcroft well enough to feel his pain on being the first man in history to lose a Senate seat to a dead man. What I did know, however, was the number count in the U.S. Senate, too close for comfort in terms of maintaining a Republican majority.

That in mind, I forwarded my rusty legal advice (not having practiced since Eisenhower was president) on what the senator might do to stop the nationwide laughter at his expense. It didn't require the mind of a constitutional scholar, I told Ashcroft's friend, to understand that when Article One, Section Three, sets out that a U.S. senator must be "an Inhabitant of the State for which he shall be chosen," the Founding Fathers didn't mean a *literal* inhabitant, six feet under. A challenge was in order.

A chuckle on the other end of the line, then: "I'll pass it on." Translated from the arcane language of Washington insiders, that meant "You're wasting my time"; which, in fact, I was, since what I'd considered a unique constitutional insight had also occurred to several dozen other Republican legal experts across the country.

But the candidate himself, as it developed, had other ideas. A few days after the election, Ashcroft let out word that he'd considered challenging the election, but following contemplation and prayer had decided against it (a first, since I'd never previously heard of a politician asking God whether he should seek high office and being told "No").

To be sure, Ashcroft's decision not to challenge the election results—there was a better-than-even chance the Supreme Court would have ruled in his favor—came as both a surprise and a disappointment to his friends, members of his Senate staff, and, needless to say, his campaign contributors, all of whom wondered about his plans for the future. At that point, the possibility that he'd be named Attorney General in a Bush administration seemed nebulous, the presidential election itself being up in the air because of Al Gore's challenge of the Florida returns.

There was, however, a Plan B. Like former Senate colleagues Bob Dole, George Mitchell, Howard Baker, and Bob Packwood, Ashcroft could add his name, experience, and cachet to the roster of a high-powered Washington law office. What money-making firm of high rollers doing business on Capitol Hill wouldn't take in John Ashcroft? He was, after all, a Yale law graduate.

When I first came to Washington in the late 1950s, it was said of members of the Senate that the only way they'd ever leave Capitol Hill, barring defeat at the polls, was in a pine box. The seniority system was in place back then. The longer you stayed, the higher you rose in committee, the more power you wielded. People spoke of "the Senate Club," the most exclusive coterie in town. To be a U.S. senator was to be part of what was then considered (if only by the members themselves) "the world's greatest deliberative body." Outside of being elevated to the White House or U.S. Supreme Court, a Senate seat was as high as a public figure could go—or would want to go—in life.

Quaint times, when corporate lobbying as we now know it was in its infancy, before K Street became a synonym for big-buck lobbying. Money back then? When I went to work for a Washington public relations firm in December 1958, I was told that if I really wanted to make a killing in town, I should stop writing speeches and get into the lobbying end of the business where, if I proved my worth, I could earn up to $100,000 a year! (Today fledgling lobbyists straight out of law school can begin at $150,000 a year; congressional staffers who move their Rolodex files from the Hill to K Street lobbying firms start at anywhere from $200,000 to $300,000 annually.)

Three changes that came about in the next two decades would diminish the value John Ashcroft and his colleagues placed on membership in the Senate Club: First, the exponential growth of the lobbying industry and its need for those with "access" to government policymakers opened the way for ex-senators to make, in Ashcroft's words, "significant multiples" of what they had earned. Second, the end of the congressional seniority system and rotation of committee chairmanships reduced the power and prestige that once went with being a Senate elder. Third—back to money—the unrelenting demand on a senator's time to raise campaign funds just to stay in office became onerous for all but the independently wealthy. In even a small state like Maryland, the Senate candidate without ten to fifteen million dollars in hand is underfunded. In states like New York and California, it would be cheaper to buy a paradise island in the South Pacific and set yourself up as monarch-for-life than to run for the Senate.[1]

Better to be on the outside of the system, making money, than on the inside trying to raise it. Though he'd spent his entire life as an insider, first as Missouri's attorney general, then as its governor and U.S. senator, by the year 2000 John Ashcroft was ready to move on. Losing his Senate seat to a dead man could turn out to be a blessing in disguise. When the President-elect called to offer him the job of Attorney General, Ashcroft, after a dutiful prayer session, snapped it up. There was power to wield as Attorney General, more than he'd ever had as one senator out of a hundred. The riches of K Street could wait. They'd still be there when he finished his job at the DOJ.

Meanwhile, there were other good, worshipful Republicans around to take advantage of the new entrepreneurial prospects opened up by the party's holding the whip hand on both ends of Pennsylvania Avenue, from the Caucus Room to the Oval Office...

* * *

Headline, *Washington Post*, September 20, 2005
"Bush Official Arrested in Corruption Probe"

---

[1] The same situation prevails in the House, where retired committee chairmen like Louisiana's Billy Tauzin and voter-rejected candidates like Oklahoma's Steve Largent moved on to eight-figure-per-annum lobbying jobs with major trade associations. A July 2005 study by the Congress Watch division of the organization Public Citizen found that nearly half of the 198 members of the Senate and House who've left Capitol Hill since 1998 are now registered lobbyists.

The Bush administration's top federal procurement official resigned Friday and was arrested yesterday, accused of lying and obstructing a criminal investigation into Republican lobbyist Jack Abramoff's dealings with the federal government. It was the first criminal complaint filed against a government official in the ongoing corruption probe related to Abramoff's activities in Washington.

George W. Bush came to town in January 2001, promising to change the political culture of Washington. Mission accomplished: We now have the most corrupt government, White House to Capitol Hill, in the history of the country, including or excluding the moral corruption and hypocrisy uncovered after "conservative" pederast Mark Foley was forced to resign from the House in the fall of 2006.

But I exaggerate. I wasn't around when Ulysses S. Grant or Warren Gamaliel Harding was president, so let's leave it at the most corrupt government in my lifetime.

Clinton?

He was orally serviced by an intern and used the Lincoln bedroom as a Comfort Inn for overnight stays by his fat-cat contributors, but we're talking here about *corruption*, not penny-ante Arkansas venality. (Oh yes, there was that obscene spate of last-minute presidential pardons as Bubba left the White House, but that was to raise money for his Clinton Library and we've yet to see what Dubya will do to raise money for his imperial edifice. It would have been so simple if Kenny-boy Lay hadn't screwed up.)

Nixon?

Let me tell you, there are things that have taken place in the Bush-Cheney White House that Nixon would have gagged at, not because he thought they were wrong, but because they were so blatant.

> Fantasy Excerpt, Nixon White House Tape (undated):
>
> *President:* What's this I read in the morning news summary about an energy task force?
> *Bob Haldeman:* Oh, that. John [Ehrlichman] and I didn't want to bother you with it, China on your mind and all. We called all the oil and gas lobbyists in to help draw up an energy bill. Nothing to worry about.
> *President:* Called lobbyists together? Where?
> *Haldeman:* Where else? Here.
> *President:* Here? In the White House? Lobbyists writing an energy bill? Jesus [expletive] Christ, you stupid [expletive] are gonna get me impeached!

No, not Clinton, not Nixon, but Bush-Cheney; as I say, the most corrupt government in my lifetime. Not an easy thing to swallow if you're among those who helped put it in power but not a hard case to make once you remove your rose-tinted shades and see what's taken place on both ends of Pennsylvania avenue.

Where to start? Capitol Hill? They're falling like dominoes up there, all those squeaky-clean Gingrichites who came to town in the mid-'90s to straighten up the mess left by Dan Rostenkowski and his venal Democratic colleagues. (Who was it that said it took the Democrats four decades to produce the moral squalor on the Hill that Republicans have produced in one?)

Danny Rostenkowski and his House post office scam—went to prison for a few miserable kickbacks. You want to do it the Right way, think BIG, Texas-style, like the good Lord's Scripture-spouting man-on-the-Hill, Tom ("The Hammer") DeLay. It was Tom, you'll recall, who launched the money-churning "K Street Project," aimed at leveling the competitive playing field between hungry Republican and fat Democratic lobbyists; "leveling," in DeLay's Manichean world, meaning to flatten not only the field but the Democratic opposition as well, as in his prize staff member Michael Scanlon's noted email on how to deal with a political opponent: "You kick him until he passes out, beat him over the head with a baseball bat, roll him up in an old rug, and throw him off a cliff into the pounding surf below!"

Whether Scanlon acquired that Good Samaritan mindset while attending sessions of Tom DeLay's Bible class I can't say. His two years as DeLay's official House spokesman did, however, make him a prime beneficiary of the Hammer's "Weez gonna get rich!" K Street Project, linking his fortunes to those of Jack Abramoff, the gutter lobbyist DeLay once called "one of my closest and dearest friends."

Working as a team (they dubbed their partnership "Gimme Five"), Abramoff and Scanlon would earn extraordinary fees lobbying on behalf of sweatshop factory owners in the Northern Marianas and casino-rich Indian tribes in Louisiana and Texas.[2]

They saw themselves as super-lobbyists, sponsoring lavish golfing trips to Scotland and the South Pacific for key congressional figures; jetting Hill staffers to the Super Bowl; investing in cruise ships, beachfront mansions, private planes; and, in short order, emerging as poster boys for a new breed of young Republican money-hustlers with a world view and lifestyle far removed from Barry Goldwater's vision of a conservative ethic focused on "the whole man, not the material man."

---

[2] The felonious adventures of Jack and Mike have been fairly well documented in the mainstream (if not the Fox-stream) media, but their Indian casino caper deserves special attention, if only because it has the ring of a Mel Brooks farce in the telling: In racking up some $45 million in lobbying fees from various casino-owning Indian tribes in Louisiana and Texas, Abramoff and Scanlon in one case paid the Christian Coalition ethicist Ralph Reed to crusade for the shutdown of a Texas Indian casino, then hustled the tribe into paying them $4.2 million to lobby Congress to *reopen* it! (How do you say "chutzpah" in Coushatta Indian?)

Chapter 10

HARDING WAS A PIKER

"I think he's been dealt the worst, rawest deal I've ever seen in my life. Words like bribery are being used to describe things that happened every day in Washington and are not bribes."

—CONGRESSMAN DANA ROHRABACHER (R, CALIFORNIA), DEFENDING HIS
FRIEND JACK ABRAMOFF

"I gave that guy ten grand and he voted against me!"

—JACK ABRAMOFF, EXPRESSING HIS DISAPPOINTMENT
ABOUT ANOTHER CONGRESSIONAL FRIEND

IMAGINE THE TEAPOT DOME scandal taking place under the administration of Theodore Roosevelt or the Watergate break-in and cover-up occurring in the Eisenhower years.

Impossible. The pieces don't fit, unless you're living in an alternate universe.

Not that there weren't venal or thuggish Washington operatives around in those years—there always have been and always will be. But it's the leader, always the leader, who by direct or indirect political body language sets the bar for ethical and moral standards in his administration, whether high or low.

George W. Bush seems to have some limited understanding of that truism—why else would he insist on a dress code for members of his White House staff? No exceptions, no waivers. Be assured that if David Safavian, second-ranking official in the White House Office of Management and Budget, had come to work without a tie the day he was indicted on corruption charges, he would have heard about it from either the White House chief of staff or Dubya himself. But as to why Safavian, a lobbying protégé of Jack Abramoff, was ever hired by the White House in the first place...

One bad apple slipping through the White House personnel screening process? An aberration? If we were talking about some low- or medium-level drudge working in the catacombs of the Eisenhower Executive Office Building, that might be the case. But David Safavian was no drudge. He was the one man, out of hundreds qualified for the job, the White House hired to hand out billions of dollars appropriated by Congress for reconstruction in New Orleans and other Gulf coast areas hit by Hurricane Katrina.[1]

---

[1] In June 2006, Safavian was convicted by a federal jury for lying and obstructing justice in covering up his efforts to assist Abramoff in acquiring two properties controlled by the General Services Administration. The cover-up involved a lavish golfing trip to St. Andrews in Scotland sponsored by Abramoff. Others on the trip included Congressman Bob Ney, who later resigned his office and pleaded guilty to taking bribes from Abramoff, and the always available Ralph Reed.

Nor was Safavian the only close business associate of Jack Abramoff to be hired for a top-level position in the Bush-Cheney White House. Consider the odds on this "aberration": Karl Rove, arguably the most powerful un-elected official in George W.'s White House, was looking for an executive assistant to run his office. Quick guess as to how many experienced candidates on Capitol Hill and in other government agencies—not to mention Washington's private sector—would apply for the job if the hiring process were open? Ten thousand? Twenty?

Conceded, to be Karl Rove's executive assistant, privy to the innermost operations of the Oval Office, requires something extra in the way of know-how, so cut the number to a mere five thousand; then put the names in a hat or a barrel, draw one out and by golly, as Don Rumsfeld would say, guess who got the job?

One Susan Ralston, *Jack Abramoff's executive assistant!* There was news there, significant news, but the White House press corps, bulldogs when it comes to questioning why they're limited to one travel bag on presidential trips, somehow missed it. Had they been given a handout telling them the executive assistant to the number one sleaze on K Street would start Monday as the executive assistant to the number one political advisor to the president, someone—possibly the intrepid David Gregory of NBC-TV celebrity—might have raised an eyebrow. But no handout being offered, public awareness of Jack Abramoff's pipeline to the Bush-Cheney White House came only after a House committee investigation in September 2006.

And how did Susan Ralston make the leap from Abramoff's Indian-scamming office to 1600 Pennsylvania? An old Washington story—somebody knew somebody. In this case, Grover Norquist, who worked with Jack on the Indian casino accounts, heard that his good friend Karl needed someone to run his office and could think of no one better qualified for the job than Susan, the savvy young woman who ran Abramoff's shop.

Great idea, thought Jack. Much as he'd miss Susan, he could see how planting her—that is, having her on the other end of the line when he called Rove's office—was worth the sacrifice. The move took place in February 2001, a serendipitous arrangement that greased the way for Abramoff's lobbying team to make, according to a 2006 report of the House Government Reform Committee, some 485 business contacts with the White House over the next three years, including 82 with Rove himself.

A direct, personal tie between the most corrupt lobbyist in Washington and the man George W. Bush called "the architect" of his political career. It's obvious what Abramoff got out of it, but what about Rove?

Email from Jack Abramoff to Susan Ralston, March 2002:

"Hi, Susan. I just saw Karl and mentioned the NCAA opportunity, which he was really jazzed about. If he wants to join us in the Pollin box, please let me know as soon as you can."

The "NCAA opportunity" having been an offer by Jack of to-kill-for skybox seats in the owner's box at Washington's MCI Center when the NCAA basketball tournament came to town; to which Susan Ralston responded:

Email, Susan to Jack:

"Karl is interested in Fri. and Sun., 3 tickets for his family?"

Done, replied Abramoff, and a few days later there they were in the Pollin box, Karl, his family, and host Jack, enjoying the perks of power and privilege. But don't jump to any dark Bush-bashing conclusions: Karl *insisted* on paying for the tickets ($50 each), and all Jack got out of it was the chance to email a business colleague after the game: "He's [Karl's] a great guy. Told me anytime we needed something just to let him know through Susan."

Headline, *Washington Post,* September 23, 2005: **"Tyco Exec: Abramoff Claimed Ties to Administration"**

Republican lobbyist Jack Abramoff bragged two years ago that he was in contact with White House political aide Karl Rove on behalf of a large, Bermuda-based corporation that wanted to avoid incurring some taxes and continue receiving federal contracts according to a written statement by President Bush's nominee to be deputy attorney general.

The nominee was one Timothy E. Flanigan, yet another example of how coincidence and luck of the draw works in the hiring process used by the Bush-Cheney White House. The job of deputy attorney general that Flanigan was scheduled to fill requires overseeing the trials of white-collar felons and others charged with criminal conduct. His qualifications? Aside from having virtually no trial experience himself, Flanigan would, if confirmed, go to the Justice Department directly from Tyco International, where he held the position of general counsel. That's Tyco, the conglomerate best known in recent years for its flamboyant CEO Dennis Kozlowski, who at the time of Flanigan's nomination was serving an eight-and-a-half-year sentence for misappropriating over $400 million of company funds ($1 million of which went into his wife's fortieth birthday party).

Let's see now, the nominee has limited trial experience and serves as general counsel for an outfit whose CEO is doing hard time as a major swindler. In any other administration, Timothy Flanigan's name, far from being sent to the Senate for confirmation, would have been buried at the bottom of a wastebasket in the White House personnel office. Tim, however, had just the qualifications Attorney General Alberto Gonzales was looking for in a deputy: He made no waves, took orders like a good Prussian, and had the good sense to give his bosses exactly what they were looking for in the way of legal research; as when, while serving as Gonzales' deputy counsel in the White House (before going to Tyco), Flanigan worked with the team that drafted the infamous fifteen-page Torture Memo allowing the CIA authority to go beyond the rules set by the Geneva Conventions in the treatment of war prisoners—the memo so dear to Dick Cheney's heart in that it told proponents of the Conventions to go fuck themselves with a water board.

It was the same controversial memo that put Gonzales' own confirmation in jeopardy when his nomination as Attorney General went to the Hill. Gonzales survived the grilling but in Flanigan's case, the nominee's ties to Abramoff, added to his role in preparing the memo, were enough to sink the nomination. Back to Tyco he went, presumably to work out the company's problems with the federal government by hiring another well-wired Republican lobbyist.

* * *

Karl Rove claims Theodore Roosevelt is the 20th-century American president he most admires but like much else in the Bush-Cheney White House, Rove's talk isn't borne out by his actions. If the "architect" of George W. Bush's presidency meant what he says about TR, a chemical industry lobbyist like Gale Norton would never have served as the administration's Secretary of Interior, with an oil-drenched lobbyist like J. Stephen Griles as her assistant secretary.[2]

---

[2] Both big-time lobbyists for metal, oil, and chemical interests, Norton's primary qualifications for the job being her apprenticeship at Interior under the tree-loathing secretary James Watt during the Reagan years. ("You remember James Watt," humorist Bob Orben wrote at the time, "a voice crying in what was formerly the wilderness.") As for Griles, by all accounts his lobbying activities for oil and gas clients didn't end when he went to Interior as Morton's assistant. Jack Abramoff described him as "our guy Steve" in email reports involving his Indian casino clients.

What Karl probably sees when he thinks of Teddy Roosevelt is a commander in chief with an imperialist bent. But much as the history books dwell on TR's big-stick diplomacy, his most important legacy to his country and party might well have been his role as America's first conservationist president.

That's right, conservation was once a Republican policy preserve, with the godfather of what's known as the environmental movement a Republican appointee of the president Karl Rove most admires. Named head of the U.S. Forestry Service by Roosevelt, Gifford Pinchot was the foremost champion of preserving America's natural resources for posterity—until he was fired by TR's successor, William Howard Taft, for opposing the Taft administration's plan to turn virgin Alaskan land over to the coal industry.

The country's growing. We need more coal to meet our energy needs. So went the Taft administration's mantra. Substitute oil for coal, Bush-Cheney for Taft, and we have yet another exhibit to prove the old French axiom that tells us *Plus ça change, plus c'est la même chose.*

Except, where in today's Republican party can you find a conservationist candidate for president or a Gifford Pinchot? Someone willing to turn away campaign contributions or lose his job rather than cave in to the oil industry gluttons who'd cap the Washington Monument with a derrick if they thought the National Mall could bring home a gusher (with Dick Cheney cheering them on and Dubya manning the drill).

A stretch, you say? Maybe, but don't bet your Halliburton Preferred against it. Seven years running and this White

House has yet to see an oil rig it didn't like. Or could you be one of those corporate-lackey "conservatives" who believes the Bush-Cheney line that drilling in the Arctic National Wildlife Refuge is the long-term answer to America's dependence on Middle Eastern oil and any member of Congress who votes against it is playing into Osama bin Laden's hands?

If so, take the word of a political ancient who remembers past presidents warning that if we didn't develop a long-range energy plan—specifically *their* plan—we were turning our children's future over to long-shirted Middle Eastern sheiks. Not that the sky won't fall one day if we don't face up to our over-indulgence in oil, but the Bush-Cheney promise that drilling in the Arctic would solve the problem is the domestic equivalent of their promise that regime change in Iraq would stabilize the Middle East. Lies in both cases and lies told for much the same reason: enriching their oil industry friends, short and long term.

✳ ✳ ✳

Headline, the *Hill,* May 1, 2005:
"Ashcroft Joins K Street Legions"

"I have been at the heart of the war on terror."
—FORMER ATTORNEY GENERAL JOHN ASHCROFT, PITCHING HIS LOBBYING
SKILLS TO PROSPECTIVE CLIENTS, SPRING, 2005

John Ashcroft has left the building. The bare-breasted statue he used as a backdrop for his news conferences at the Justice Department is no longer sheathed by order of the

Attorney General. Those "voluntary" prayer sessions every morning in the AG's office are no longer mandatory for top department officials. The frantic gathering of documents to beat Homeland Security chief Tom Ridge to the cameras to announce some new threat or breakup of a terrorist ring is a thing of the past.

John, you see, is no longer *fighting* the threat of terrorism but as the first former U.S. attorney general in history to register as a lobbyist, he's *profiting* from it. "The Ashcroft Group contacted us," revealed Chuck Jones, spokesman for ChoicePoint, a company that specializes in gathering consumer data used by Justice Department investigators. "He's got a lot of knowledge that could benefit ChoicePoint."

A lot of knowledge but more important, a lot of access to the very people inside the Justice Department who hand out the lucrative contracts ChoicePoint competes for. Indeed, one of the reasons Ashcroft felt fairly confident he could land ChoicePoint as a client was that the company had already grown rich from Justice Department contracts handed out *during* his years as attorney general.

Conflict of interest? No, the man no longer holds office. Illegal? No, it all falls under the heading, as Mr. Dooley once said, of "seein' your opportunities and takin' 'em." Unethical? Please. We're talking about a man whose calls are returned by Jesus the same day.

Ashcroft, in the insouciant manner of a True Believer who conducts daily prayer sessions and therefore knows he can do no wrong, describes his new role on K Street as merely being "a lightning rod for people facing challenges."

A less charitable description would be the one applied by Republicans to Democrats who profited from access to White House officials during the Truman and Lyndon Johnson eras: influence peddling. Or, to put it in the way Barry Goldwater did on being asked whether, on leaving the Senate, he planned to open an office on K Street and go into lobbying: "No. I'm too old to be a pimp."

* * *

"I have both a very high regard for your ability and an unfaltering belief in your integrity. I had these impressions when I asked you to come into my Cabinet, and I have no reason of any kind to modify my earlier impressions concerning you as either friend or public servant."

—WARREN HARDING TO SECRETARY OF INTERIOR ALBERT FALL AFTER A SENATE INVESTIGATION EXPOSED FALL'S ROLE IN THE TEAPOT DOME SCANDAL

Poor Harding. He worked to bring "normalcy" to the country when what he really needed was a war to take the public's mind off the corruption brought on by his political appointees and cigar-smoking cronies from Ohio. Led by the architect of his administration, Attorney General Harry Daugherty, they would meet nightly at what became known as "the little red house on H Street" to talk over deals, drink illegal whiskey, and play poker. Occasionally the President would drop by, swap stories, have a drink or two, and hold a few poker hands. Harding never lost. Fool that he was, he chalked it up to shrewd card playing.

Was Harding the most corrupt president in history? It all depends, to paraphrase one of his carnally inclined successors, on the meaning of corruption. Harding himself never made a dime out of Albert Fall's or Harry Daugherty's deal making. But by his morally indolent example, he set the tone for what would be tolerated on his watch.

That Teapot Dome was simply a product of the age— the Roaring Twenties of bootleg whiskey, Wall Street swindles, and Florida real estate scams—goes with the theory that leaders are shaped by their times and if Harding hadn't been in the White House in 1921, we would have seen some other rudderless president tending a government corrupted by the Zeitgeist. But if that were the case, how to account for the scandal-free years in the nation's capital that followed Teapot Dome?

Though Calvin Coolidge bored the Algonquin Round Table and exalted the profit motive ("The business of America is business"), there is something to be said for a leader, however uncharismatic, who sets the tone for what *won't* be tolerated on his watch. One look at Silent Cal and you knew he would never be found in a little red house on H Street—or anywhere else—playing poker with deal-making lobbyists.

Whatever else history says of him, give Warren Harding this: He left behind a vice president who had a sure moral compass, a man of conservative ethics. Would that we could say the same of the "conservative" vice president now one heartbeat away from the Oval Office...

"He doesn't see the difference between public and private interest."

—USAF COLONEL SAM GARDINER (RET.) (NATIONAL WAR COLLEGE) OF DICK CHENEY'S ROLE IN THE HANDOUT OF BILLIONS OF DOLLARS IN IRAQ CONTRACTS TO HIS FORMER COMPANY, HALLIBURTON

To repeat, *the most corrupt administration in my lifetime.*

Chapter 11

CLINTON REDUX:
SYMBOLS AND SIDESHOWS

"Old Glory lost today."
—BILL FRIST ON THE U.S. SENATE'S REJECTION OF THE FLAG PROTECTION
AMENDMENT TO THE CONSTITUTION, JUNE 27, 2006

"Symbolic votes, message politics, and little serious legislation."
—BROOKINGS INSTITUTION SCHOLAR THOMAS E. MANN ON WHY CONGRESS
HAS BECOME "THE BROKEN BRANCH" OF GOVERNMENT

O THAT ECCENTRIC OLD SAM Hayakawa were still around to lecture his GOP colleagues when they make their annual run at reviving the so-called Flag Protection Amendment to the U.S. Constitution. If you're over thirty, you may recall Sam as the tam-wearing Republican senator from California in the 1970s. But quirks aside, he was also recognized as one of the preeminent semanticists of his time, the author of *Language in Thought and Action*, a text that remains, a decade and a half after his death, a classic in its field.

What would Sam—or rather, San Francisco State's Professor S. I. Hayakawa—have to say if he were on the Senate floor when Orrin Hatch rose to deliver his annual pitch on Old Glory as "our national symbol" and why its "desecration" is equivalent to spitting on the graves of all those brave Americans who fought and died at Concord, Gettysburg, the Argonne, etc.

My guess is that Sam would direct Hatch to the chapter in *Language in Thought and Action* entitled "The Symbolic Process." That's the one that warns against prizing "the symbols of piety, of civic virtue, or of patriotism above actual piety, civic virtue, or patriotism."

Not that Hayakawa's lecture would be likely to do any good. I'd just like to know there were still Republican senators around who didn't think of the people who elected them as knuckle-walking Pleistocene morons.

Don't misunderstand, Orrin; I love "our national symbol." I was on the detail that raised it the first few weeks I was on duty at Fort Jackson in 1950. Lowered and folded it, too, with due reverence and proper flag etiquette. So don't think it's because I'm unpatriotic when I say that on reading your remarks and Bill Frist's comment on losing that 2006 vote I didn't know whether to retch or change party registration. (Thanks to Senate Democratic Leader Harry Reid, my indecision didn't last. When Reid said he'd voted *for* the amendment because "I knew it wouldn't pass," I forgot about switching parties and reached for the barf bag.)

Let's see, there's the Flag Protection Amendment of 2005; the Federal Marriage Amendment of 2004; and, of course, the desperately needed Protecting the Reference to God in the Pledge of Allegiance and National Motto Amendment of 2003—all spearheaded by supposedly conservative Republicans who, while professing reverence for the U.S. Constitution, don't let a congressional day pass without devising some new way to undercut its spirit.

Gary Bauer, for example, the American Values champion, was heard to express outrage at a Republican congressman who said he opposed the Marriage Amendment because he thought marriage and family law should be left to the states. "Incredible," Bauer told his followers, "that a Republican lawmaker should think such a thing. An institution as sacred as marriage is too important to be left to the states."

Pardon? Did I miss something in my reading of *The Federalist Papers*? Could it be that those Great Society Liberals Bauer claims to despise have been right in saying the Constitution's reference to "powers reserved to the States" is so much 18th-century drivel? Or that Madison, on leaving the Constitutional Convention, walked a block, slapped his forehead and turned to Franklin to say, "Good God, Ben, we forgot to define marriage as being between a man and a woman!"

Old Glory imperiled and the institution of marriage on the eve of destruction: Symbolic non-issues to anyone other than the Betsy Ross Society and Gary Bauer's "values" constituency. But there's this to be said in their favor: Along with Britney Spears' pregnancies, *American Idol*, and sports stars on steroids, they take our minds off the war in Iraq, terrorism, illegal immigration, Social Security, deficit spending, and other real issues the White House and Congress can't, or won't, get a grip on.

The Politics of Symbolism

In 1977, I wrote a book (*P-R as in President*) that dealt with the use of spin and imagery on American presidential elections, e.g., Tony Orlando's "spontaneous" dance with Betty Ford at the 1976 Republican convention, and Jimmy Carter ostentatiously toting his own garment bag through airports.

Then came what Sidney Blumenthal called "The Permanent Campaign" and with it the spin doctors and media consultants who helped candidates get elected and stayed on to help them govern. Carter's televised "fireside chats" during an energy crisis come to mind (he wore a sweater in case we missed the point), along with Ronald Reagan's use of "symbolism" (Mike Deaver's term) to keep the Falwell-Robertson religionists in line.

But better even than Ron, the professional actor, was Blumenthal's own White House boss, Bill the Natural. From the night in 1992 when he donned Ray-Bans and played a funky saxophone on the *Arsenio Hall Show*, I knew that, if elected, Bill Clinton would raise (or lower) the Politics of Symbolism to new levels: shades-and-sax for cool young voters, hugs-and-tears for the Walton Family set.

For most conservatives, the image that Clinton conjures up is that of the lying womanizer on camera saying,

"I did not have sex with that woman...Miss Lewinsky." For me the more telling image was that of Clinton leaving Ron Brown's funeral, chatting and grinning, until he caught sight of TV cameras. Then, on cue, the face went gray and the tears came rolling.

Nothing about George W. Bush's conduct as governor of Texas led anyone to believe that as president he'd take up the Politics of Symbolism where Bill Clinton left off. The Dubya we knew despised pretense and seemed totally disinterested in anything that smacked of image-packaging by professional spin doctors and political handlers.

Flying in as a Top Gun pilot to signal mission accomplished? Delivering a packaged show-time speech in New Orleans, another Hollywood moment, in Jackson Square with the St. Louis Cathedral as a luminous backdrop? Tell me it's a Clinton clone or President Al Gore after a Florida recount. Anybody but the George W. I knew and voted for.

We've seen genuine moments, yes. The impromptu speech at Ground Zero and the formal address at the National Cathedral following 9/11 were anything but contrived. That was Dubya as his father's son: When George H. W. shed tears while visiting a veterans' hospital or comforting bereaved parents, they were genuine tears. The old man's inability to show false emotion or do political shtick was a major factor in his losing his race for a second term; a point no doubt drilled home by Karl Rove in selling young George on the power of symbolism.

But whatever the cause—Rove's influence or some other id-altering political incubus on the White House grounds—the Governor of Texas who once thought of Bill

Clinton as "a bullshit artist" and "Three-Dollar Bill" had second thoughts after arriving in the Oval Office. The Clinton playbook—leadership by symbols and sideshows—would become his playbook as well.

✷ ✷ ✷

"The good news is—and it's hard for some to see it now—is that out of this chaos is going to come a fantastic Gulf Coast, like it was before. Out of the rubble of Trent Lott's house—he lost his entire house—there's going to be a fantastic house. And I'm looking forward to sitting on the porch."

—PRESIDENT BUSH ON TOUR, RE THE DESTRUCTION WROUGHT BY
HURRICANE KATRINA, SEPTEMBER 2, 2005

Symbolism with a tin ear. Left on his own—the speech was impromptu, unscripted—our "compassionate conservative" president picks as symbolic of thousands of coastal homes devastated by Katrina none other than Trent Lott's mansion by the sea. Moments later, confirming the fact that he hadn't given the matter much thought (you've seen one hurricane, you've seen 'em all), Bush would sum up his administration's post-Katrina effort with the all-too-memorable words, "Brownie, you're doin' a heckuva job."

Fantastic. Nothing like a public pat on the back from the boss to boost employee morale when the company's going through a rough patch: A medal to George Tenet for doin' a heckuva job spotting Saddam's WMDs, the presidency of the World Bank to Paul Wolfowitz for bringing democracy to the Middle East. What Pat

Moynihan, were he still around, might call Defining Competence Downward.

Words of praise, however, were all FEMA Director Michael Brown would get from his feckless boss. No medal, no promotion. The administration's failure to react quickly to the televised scenes of human suffering caused by Katrina required a scapegoat and a mid-level appointee like "Brownie" filled the bill perfectly. That his superior, Homeland Security Secretary Michael Chertoff, shared equal if not greater responsibility for the administration's failure made no difference. As a Cabinet member, Chertoff was inside the ring, too close to the President to be scapegoated.[1]

Accountability: another of the words of convenience used by George W. in the 2000 campaign that proved to

---

[1] Of all the thoughtless lines and phrases Bush has uttered in his years as President ("Bring it on!" and "Dead or alive"), his frat-boy reference to "Brownie" produced far-and-away the greatest political repercussion, putting the spotlight not only on Michael Brown's competence as FEMA director but, by extension, the administration's hire-a-crony process of appointments to high and mid-level positions. A few weeks later, the White House press corps homed in on Julie Myers, Bush's thirty-six-year-old nominee to head the U.S. Immigration and Customs Enforcement Agency, a government bureau operating with 20,000 employees on a $4-billion-a-year budget. Ms. Myers' qualifications for the job of heading one of the lead agencies in the government's antiterrorism program? One year as a federal prosecutor, one year as an assistant secretary at the Department of Commerce, sixteen months working for Kenneth Starr, and two years working in the White House personnel office where, obviously, she kept a sharp eye out for high-level job openings. Still not convinced she's qualified? Then try this: Ms. Myers's uncle is Air force General Richard B. Myers, chairman of the Joint Chiefs of Staff at the time of her appointment. (He was the fellow in the blue uniform who in the early days of the Iraq war used to stand next to Don Rumsfeld at news conferences with a rubber stamp in hand.) Want still more? She's married to Michael Chertoff's chief of staff. Croneyism? *Naaahh*...Dubya sees it as family values.

be "mere campaign rhetoric." As we learned after Abu Ghraib, when the Bush-Cheney White House promises to "get to the bottom" of government misconduct, it means just that, and no more. At or near the bottom is where the buck stops, with top-level officials left untouched: first, there's low-level scapegoating and a generous coat of white-wash applied by the president's spin doctors; then, if the problem still won't go away, blame it on a vast Left-wing conspiracy planned by partisan Democrats and their fellow travelers in the mainstream media.

It was a fail-proof system of damage control when the adverse publicity centered on the war against terror-ism or the eroding situation in Iraq. But the sight of hungry, homeless families in the Superdome and lifeless bodies in the streets of an American city was more than even the best White House spin machine in history could deal with.

Overnight, the symbolic image of the president rallying the nation at Ground Zero was replaced in the public mind by the White House photo of a detached George W. Bush looking down on a flooded city from the insulated comfort of his cabin aboard Air Force One. What followed, after pollsters reported a precipitous drop in Dubya's approval numbers, was a series of feel-your-pain visits to the area, complete with contrived photo-ops of a "compassionate" President surrounded by carefully auditioned African American huggables. Everything staged and scripted, down to that backlit scene in the heart of the French Quarter where the Commander in Chief would deliver a full-throated promise that "This great city will rise again."

The only thing missing was the crocodile tears.[2]

Ecologists have warned for years that the ongoing erosion of southern Louisiana's Cajun country, at the rate of twenty-five square miles a year, would in time leave New Orleans vulnerable to the most destructive effects of a high-category hurricane. "There's a reason they're called 'barrier' islands," marine biologist Kerry St. Pé told travel writer Mike Tidwell in 2002. "This is the first line of defense against hurricanes. Without these islands, a hurricane's storm surge will slam right into the coast unchecked...Then it's straight into the population centers. I'm afraid it might be really, really ugly" (Tidwell, *Bayou Farewell: The Rich Life and Tragic Death of Louisiana's Cajun Coast*).

Ugly indeed. But it seems a Bush-Cheney administration that pours tens of billions of dollars into restoring the "infra-structure" of post-Saddam Iraq, can't afford to "dedicate large resources" to our own country's coastline "at a time of large federal budget deficits." A cynic might suggest that Louisianians should find some way for Halliburton to get into the act. Somehow, I'm sure, the resources would not only be found but also dispersed via no-bid contracts.

---

[2] What made Bush's promise of a "fantastic" Gulf Coast ring especially false was the fact that little more than a month before Katrina his secretary of energy, Samuel Bodham, had brusquely informed Louisianians that the administration could not afford to "dedicate large resources" to help restore the state's coastline "at a time of large federal budget deficits" ("Bush Plan Erodes Aid for Louisiana Coast," *New Orleans Times-Picayune*, July 23, 2005).

A confession of special interest here: For all the years I've spent in Washington, New Orleans is the home I knew and loved as a boy: Mardi Gras parades, swimming in Lake Pontchartrain on summer afternoons, fishing with my father in Plaquemines, po' boys, Elmer's chocolate, and seven-cent streetcar fares (yes, I go back that far).

I am, in sum, a consummate New Orleanian, with all the ingrained cynicism about politics and government that implies. On a psychiatrist's couch it would probably come out that growing up in Louisiana rather than reading Edmund Burke or Russell Kirk was what led me to Barry Goldwater's brand of conservatism.

For a while there, when he was more his father's son than Karl Rove's client, I thought I saw a little of that genuine brand on George W. I should have known better. I can imagine Barry Goldwater doing many things were he president at a time when a Category Five hurricane hit the Gulf Coast, but symbolic speeches and hug-a-voter sideshows wouldn't be among them.

Spinning Goldwater: "I Don't Run Trains"

Vintage Barry, 1964: We were on a whistle-stop tour, campaigning by train as another presidential underdog, Harry Truman, had done sixteen years before. All went well the first three days, apart from our candidate, a former World War II pilot, being less than pleased about jolting along in a passenger train while his preferred mode of travel, a Boeing 727, sat idle at Dulles National Airport. Nor did his mood improve when asked by the president of the railroad, a rock-solid Republican, to pose for a press picture in the cab of the train while wearing an engineer's cap.

Unfortunately, I was the staff member assigned to set up the photo shoot, which meant lining up the cameramen during a thirty-minute layover in Lima, Ohio, leading a less-than-willing presidential candidate to the train's cab, seating him at the angle the cameramen preferred, and then handing him the cap.

Problem: No one had told him about the cap.

"What the hell is this for?"

"The cap, Senator, they said they wanted you—"

"Wanted me what? To wear the goddamn thing? Here, you keep it. I'm a pilot, I don't run trains."

And that's the way the shoot went down. (I still have the cap.)

Chapter 12

THE SINCLAIR LEWIS PRESIDENCY

"Experience should teach us to be most on our guard to protect liberty when the government's purposes are beneficent. Men born to freedom are naturally alert to repel invasion of their liberty by evil-minded rulers. The greatest dangers to liberty lurk in insidious encroachment by men of zeal, well-meaning but without understanding."

—JUSTICE LOUIS BRANDEIS, DISSENT, *OLMSTEAD V. U.S.* (1928)

I F YOU'RE A BABY BOOMER, you probably haven't read *It Can't Happen Here*. If you're a member of Generation X, Y, or Z, you've probably never heard of it, or of its author, Sinclair Lewis, for that matter, though he was the first American novelist ever to win a Nobel Prize for literature.

As political novels go, the book is a minor classic. But

since your deconstructionist liberal arts professors didn't get around to teaching 20th-century American literature, and it's doubtful anything written in 1935 would make the final cut in Oprah's book selections, let me fill you in on the book and its author.

To begin, it's the first political fiction in the 20th century to take a dark view of America's future as the land of the free and the home of the brave. "Red" Lewis, you see (it was his hair color, not his politics that earned him the nickname), was one of those social misanthropes Bill O'Reilly and Ann Coulter are forever railing against on Fox News, the kind of anti-establishment contrarian who couldn't see the national glass as anything but half empty, and cracked at that. His novel *Main Street* satirized the banality of middle-American boosterism, and its sequel *Babbitt* mocked what he saw as the self-satisfied philistinism of a middle-American booster. As if those two novels weren't enough to get his works banned in Boston and Peoria, in 1927 *Elmer Gantry* savaged the latent hypocrisy of the evangelical ministry of that era.

Growing up in Huey Long's Louisiana, I fastened onto *It Can't Happen Here* during my days at Fortier High (where Huey's son Russell went to school), just as ten years later I couldn't pass up Robert Penn Warren's *All the King's Men* while at Tulane. (That one you may have heard of. Sean Penn played the lead role in 2005's dismal remake of the movie.)

Both novels were built around a central character—a charismatic country boy come to power—patterned after Long, the U.S. senator from Louisiana who in the mid-'30s was called by President Roosevelt "one of the two most dangerous men in America" (General Douglas MacArthur was number two on FDR's list).

The character Lewis drew from Huey was Senator Berzelius (Buzz) Windrip, a stem-winding demagogue swept into the White House during the Depression '30s, a time when Americans were looking for a leader, as Lewis framed his story, not only to find work but to save their souls. He would promise to do both, but at the cost of their freedom.

A satirist who wrote with a heavy though sure hand, Lewis was anything but subtle in getting his message across. Two years before *It Can't Happen Here* was published, Adolf Hitler had come to power, promising both economic and spiritual salvation for the German people. Buzz Windrip was Lewis's idea of the form an American Hitler would take, with the America we know overrun by Storm Troopers (Minutemen, Lewis called them), and littered with concentration camps for the disposition of enemies of the state.

Though no ideologue, Lewis in this case bought into the dark Leftist vision of an America susceptible if not eager to embrace a Right-wing dictatorship. The author of *It Can't Happen Here*, who cynically believed that it could, was wrong for his time, but not because he misread the latent possibility that the American people could one day fall under some form of totalitarianism. Lewis was simply off the mark in thinking it would come about through the rabble-rousing demagoguery of a Midwestern Buzz Windrip, rather than the smug banality of a sagebrush George Babbitt with an Elmer Gantry running his White House Office of Faith-based Initiatives.

* * *

"The contest for ages has been to rescue liberty from the grasp of executive power."

—DANIEL WEBSTER

"I believe in a strong, robust executive authority and I think that the world we live in demands it."

—CO-PRESIDENT DICK CHENEY, DECEMBER 20, 2005

Leading up to the crucial midterm elections of 2006 there lodged in the veritable bowels of the Bush-Cheney White House an academic hit man hired by Karl Rove to work up diatribes against critics of the Iraq war. His name was Peter Wehner, his title The Director of the Office of Strategic Initiatives (nice Orwellian touch). Among his notable contributions to the White House case for war was an April 2006 op-ed piece for the *Wall Street Journal* in which he assailed William F. Buckley and George Will for having fallen out of goose step with what he termed the administration's "freedom agenda."

Wehner's argument in favor of staying the course in Iraq was that "our own democratic development—which included the Articles of Confederation and a 'fiery trial' that cost more than 600,000 American lives—should remind critics that we must somehow be patient with others." To which the antiwar editors of the *American Conservative* acidly replied: "No word (from the White House) on whether we plan to remain in Iraq for the 89 years that elapsed between the Articles and the end of the Civil War."

Comparing "our own democratic development" to what's now going on in Iraq—Ahmed Chalabi as the Samuel Adams of Baghdad—plays into a theory I have that there's a low-level nerd in George W. Bush's White House who does nothing but dredge up historical analogies to buttress the administration's infirm case for invading and occupying Iraq. Strained historical analogies, but the exercise does have its instructive moments:

- If he hadn't compared impatient Iraq war critics to impatient critics of General Grant during the siege of Vicksburg, I'd never have known Donald Rumsfeld could ever find anything good to say about a hard-ass general with an unbuttoned tunic and the smell of whiskey on his breath.

- If he hadn't compared querulous critics of his administration's war policy to umbrella-carrying appeasers of Adolf Hitler, I'd never have known Dick Cheney had cut off extraterrestrial contact with Darth Vader and was now channeling Winston Churchill.

The risk you run trying to beat down your critics by citing historical precedent, however, is that two can play the analogy game. Raising the specter of Hitler in the 1930s, for instance, could lead a querulous critic to take a close look at the Bush-Cheney "freedom agenda," and come up with a counter-analogy, say, along these baleful lines:

- In the twelve years he ruled Germany as an absolute dictator, Hitler ironically operated within a constitution that journalist/historian William L. Shirer called "the most liberal and democratic document of its kind the 20th century had ever seen."

The Weimar Constitution of 1919—never repealed, even after the Nazis took power—was indeed "liberal and democratic"; and yet, as Shirer also wrote in *The Rise and Fall of The Third Reich*, it contained a loophole large enough to drive a panzer tank through. Under Article 48, called the Emergency Decree provision, the head of government, through his Minister of Justice, could suspend all civil liberties in the event of a threat to national security; which, as history tells us, is precisely what Hitler did when, shortly after he came to power, a terrorist torched the Reichstag.

Fast forward six decades:

Headline and Excerpt, the *Washington Times,* December 20, 2005:
**"Gonzales Backs Wiretaps
Says President Has Authority for Surveillance"**
by Guy Taylor

Attorney General Alberto R. Gonzales yesterday said President Bush has "inherent authority" to conduct secret surveillance inside the United States without getting a warrant from any judicial body.

The administration has been authorized to intercept phone calls and gather "signals intelligence" without warrants since shortly after September 11, when Congress authorized the president to "use all necessary and appropriate force" to combat terrorism.

"We believe the president also has the inherent authority under the Constitution, as commander in chief, to engage in this kind of activity," Mr. Gonzales added. "Signals intelligence has been a fundamental aspect of waging war since the Civil War."

It's all constitutional, you see, with yet another Civil War analogy to back it up. The Bush-Cheney White House may not have learned the lesson of Vietnam but this wiretapping, torture-friendly administration isn't about to make the same mistake Dick Nixon made when he authorized, then covered up, wiretaps during the Watergate years. Why cover up when you can put a legal ferret on the executive payroll to sniff out the Article 48 in the U.S. Constitution?

The Yoo Doctrine

Excerpt of debate between John Yoo, former Justice Department legal counsel, and Professor Douglas

Cassel, Notre Dame Law School, December 1, 2005:

Cassel: If the President deems that he's got to torture somebody, including by crushing the testicles of the person's child, there is no law that can stop him?
Yoo: No treaty.
Cassel: Also no law of Congress. That is what you wrote in the August 2002 memo.
Yoo: I think it depends on why the President thinks he can do that.

Meet John Yoo, architect of the legal framework used by Alberto Gonzales when he went before Congress to justify warrantless wiretaps and by Dick Cheney when he posits the Geneva Conventions don't apply to prisoners in the war on terror.

A Korean American whose parents emigrated to the United States when he was three months old, Yoo, with his Harvard-Yale law pedigree and grounded view of an all-powerful Chief Executive, would have been a perfect fit for a White House slot during the Kennedy-Johnson years. As it was, arriving in Washington forty years later, he would find a comfortable niche as the Neo-Con authority on bugging and torture in the Bush-Cheney administration.

It was the forty-year-old Yoo, then serving as counsel in John Ashcroft's Justice Department, who wrote the post-9/11 memorandum assuring the White House that "the president's broad military power to use military force to defend the nation…would allow [him] to take *whatever actions he deems appropriate to preempt or respond to terrorist threats from new quarters*" (emphasis supplied).

Repeat: *whatever actions he deems appropriate*…and there you have it, robust as even a Dick Cheney could ask for, Article 48 translated from the German; an interpretation of the U.S. Constitution, as Supreme Court Justice Sandra Day O'Connor scathingly noted, that makes "a state of war a blank check for the president when it comes to the rights of the nation's citizens."

Blank check; yes, that's exactly what John Yoo intended. The fact that Sandra Day O'Connor proved to be soft on terrorism merely shows how right Yoo's professed intellectual idol Robert Bork is when he says our courts need a purgative and the country as a whole is slouching toward Gomorrah.

"The worst thing you could do [when] people are critical of your views is run and hide. I agree with the work I did. I'm one of the few people willing to defend decisions I made in government."

—JOHN YOO, QUOTED IN THE *WASHINGTON POST* BENEATH THE HEADLINE "SCHOLAR STANDS BY POST-9/11 WRITINGS ON TORTURE, DOMESTIC EAVESDROPPING," DECEMBER 26, 2005

Never apologize, never explain: a man after Dick Cheney's own heart. But why should we expect anything less from a macho scholar who thinks so far out of the box he can read nut-crushing into the President's power to wage war under Article II, Section 2, of the U.S. Constitution?[1]

* * *

Two questions come to mind: First, unless six years of Bush-Cheneyism have Orwellized the word to mean its exact opposite, how does an authoritarian advocate of one-man rule come to call himself a conservative? The idea of a limited, rather than a "robust" executive authority—a principle rooted in the Constitution and the *Federalist Papers*—lies at the heart of modern conservatism, dating back to the Roosevelt '30s.

Second, has it occurred to others who call themselves conservative and yet support the Cheney-Yoo notion of unlimited presidential authority that the powers assumed by this administration will automatically transfer to the next? Or has the possibility of a President Hillary operating as a "strong, robust" executive never crossed their "conservative" minds?

---

[1] Though John Yoo was the legal guru behind the White House defense of wiretapping and torture, it was Dick Cheney's office that pushed the idea of expanding presidential power by the use of "signing statements" attached to bills passed by Congress (the listing of presidential objections to legislation the President has nominally signed and approved). The Bush-Cheney White House isn't the first to use such statements, but no previous White House employed them as liberally—800 times and counting as of January 2007. In effect, a presidential signing statement tells the Congress, "Though as president I'm not going to veto this bill, I don't necessarily have to abide by its provisions." As chairman of the Senate Judiciary Committee, Senator Arlen Specter (R, Pennsylvania) in early 2006 condemned such statements as "blatant encroachments" on congressional authority. If the Bush-Cheney White House keeps abusing the practice, said Specter, "there may as well not be a Congress." This, in case Specter and his congressional colleagues haven't yet caught on, is precisely what the Vice President has in mind.

Headline, *Slate Press Box,*
March 13, 2006:
"O'Connor Forecasts Dictatorship"

There goes Sandra Day O'Connor again, making waves in a lecture at Georgetown University. Jerry Falwell warned us she'd be a pain if the Senate confirmed her nomination, but nobody listened. Now she's an ex-justice claiming, in remarks one listener described as "dripping with sarcasm," that unless Republicans stop their judge-bashing, the country's headed for a "dictatorship."

No, it's not George W.'s Supreme Court appointments that led her to the "d" word. It's the Coulter-like rhetoric of Republicans on Capitol Hill, scapegoating the judiciary for all the nation's ills.

Let me confess that in my time I've done my share of judge-bashing, but going back to *Marbury v. Madison* and *Dred Scott,* who (other than the judges themselves) hasn't? It's an old American habit, indulged in by Republicans and Democrats alike.

Political elders (like the writer) recall the popular backlash in 1937 when President Roosevelt, angered by a conservative majority that was blocking his New Deal economic package, proposed increasing the size of the Supreme Court to fifteen members. The additional six members would be his appointees, of course, tipping the balance on the court his way.

FDR's court-packing plan, seen as a blatant move to nullify the independence of the judicial branch, was denounced by Republicans and Democrats alike. It would be a first step, charged conservative leaders like Ohio Senator Robert Taft, toward a one-party dictatorship. Justice O'Connor, according to those who attended her Georgetown lecture, alluded to it as a forerunner of what Republicans like Senator John Cornyn and former House Leader Tom DeLay have been up to in their attacks on the judicial system in recent years.

It was Cornyn—a Texan close enough to George W. Bush to have been on the short list to replace O'Connor when she retired—who took the floor of the Senate in April 2005 to wonder aloud whether the "raw political or ideological decisions" made by "activist judges" hadn't been the cause of a series of violent acts directed against the judiciary because of the (Cornyn's words) "great distress" they visited on the American people.

But it was the travesty of the Republican Congress' intervention in the Terri Schiavo case that drew most of O'Connor's scorn. Having forced a federal court to take jurisdiction over a case it had previously turned away, DeLay and his radical Theo-Con following turned vicious when the court's decision didn't go their way: "The men responsible for Terri Schiavo's death," warned DeLay, "will have to answer for their behavior."

It was of a piece with the prevailing *our-way-or-else* philosophy that informs the radical Theo-Con approach to governance—an approach that leaves no room for constitutional refinements like separation of powers and judicial independence when they run afoul of the Good Book.

Nothing so exposes the inner contradictions—let's call it by its Biblical name, hypocrisy—of the Theo-Con ideologue as his fork-tongued pronouncements on the federal court system: Cornyn, DeLay, and their Theo-Con colleagues (including the one in the White House) continue to rail against "activist judges"; yet, in *Schiavo*, they forcibly intervened to make federal judges who'd ruled themselves *out* of a case take it anyway, and then proceeded to denounce them for their *in*activism in refusing to overrule the Florida courts.

The hypocrisy compounds when Theo-Cons base their case against federal judges on their being, in Robert Bork's words, "an unelected, unrepresentative, unaccountable committee of lawyers applying no will but their own"; that is, ignoring the will of the people. But if the will of the people is expressed in a way Bork and the Religious Right disagree with, what then? Just this: The Yoo Doctrine applies and a "strong, robust executive" in Washington steps in to set the people straight. One example:

Oregonians in the mid-1990s twice went to the polls to approve a "Death with Dignity Act" that would permit physician-assisted suicide, an expression of popular will that John Ashcroft could hardly wait to throttle when he took over the Justice Department in 2001. One problem: There was no legislation that would allow the federal government to step in and overturn the Oregon law, a technicality Ashcroft was well aware of since, as a U.S. senator, he'd tried to push through federal legislation overriding the Oregon act and failed.

That, however, bothered Attorney General Ashcroft not at all. No specific federal law on the books that would support a federal suit to abrogate a state law voted in by popular referendum? Then we'll dredge one up to fit the occasion—the Controlled Substances Act of 1970. It was a spandex stretch of legislative intent that five years later would be rejected by a 6-3 vote of the "unelected, unrepresentative committee of lawyers" otherwise known as the U.S. Supreme Court.

Judicial restraint, by my conservative definition: The Supreme Court refusing to interpret a federal law in a way that would override the will of the people of a sovereign state. Isn't that what the Bush White House and "strict constructionists" like Robert Bork have been calling for all these years?

No question. Yet look again to see who lined up with professed strict-constructionist Justices Scalia and Thomas in support of John Ashcroft's "pro-life" motivated power grab. None other than "strict constructionist" John Roberts, taking part in his first case as Chief Justice: A harbinger of what we can expect when similar cases on the Theo-Con agenda come before the Roberts Court.

Chapter 13

WHAT WOULD BARRY DO?

"I told [President] Johnson and old colleagues on Capitol Hill that we had two clear choices. Either win the war in a relatively short time, say within a year, or pull out all our troops and come home."

—BARRY GOLDWATER RE THE VIETNAM WAR, CIRCA 1964, FROM *GOLDWATER* BY BARRY M. GOLDWATER WITH JACK CASSERLY

JOHN MCCAIN, STILL RUNNING after all these years, likes to assume the mantle of an Arizona Maverick to project the image of a Barry Goldwater for the 21st century. No disrespect for a certified Vietnam War hero, but let's, for the sake of polemic clarity, make a distinction between McCain-the-War-Hero and McCain-the-Politician.

To the point, I knew and worked for Barry Goldwater. Barry Goldwater was a friend of mine. And believe me,

John McCain is no Barry Goldwater. There are a score of reasons I could cite to back up that opinion but two should suffice, one a matter of domestic politics, the second a matter of foreign policy.

Both Goldwater and McCain at one point in their political careers crossed swords with holy-rolling Jerry Falwell, Goldwater taking the Moral Majority leader on after Falwell criticized Sandra Day O'Connor's appointment to the Supreme Court. What Falwell said at the time, that "good Christians" should oppose O'Connor because of her equivocal position on abortion, brought on the famous Goldwater retort that "Every good Christian ought to kick Falwell right in the ass." In McCain's case, Falwell's bitter opposition to his presidential candidacy in 2000 brought on a post–South Carolina primary denunciation of the Virginia televangelist as an "agent of intolerance."

Barry, despite being pressured by Republican friends to patch things up with Falwell, never recanted his remark or changed his position that Falwell and other members of what he called "the checkbook clergy" were antithetical to conservative principles. McCain, on the other hand, panting hard after the Republican presidential nomination of 2008, found it expedient in the spring of 2006 to slip into designer hair shirt and travel to Lynchburg, Virginia, to pay obeisance to the Reverend on Falwell's home turf.[1]

---

[1] This wasn't the first time that John McCain shifted into reverse gear over something he said (or didn't say) in the heat of a political campaign. During the South Carolina Republican primary of 2000, a major media issue developed over how both George W. Bush and McCain felt about the Confederate flag flying above the state capitol in Columbia. Though deplored outside the South, flying the "Stars and Bars" over the state capitol was overwhelmingly popular among Republicans likely to vote in the South Carolina presidential

All for a good cause, according to McCain's political strategists: Given the makeup of the Republican base these days, there's no way a candidate can win a GOP nomination without the support of the Religious Right. No argument there, but since the candidate in this case claims to be the second coming of Barry Goldwater, it's fair to ask whether Barry, much as he wanted the Republican presidential nomination, would have made the same pilgrimage.

The answer? Let me put it this way: What Barry said about Falwell was that every good Christian should *kick* his ass, not kiss it. Recalling Goldwater's refusal to bend or mend his ways as part of an overall campaign strategy ("He's writing the book on how not to run for president," wrote columnist Robert Novak), I wouldn't want to be the staff member who suggested he kowtow to a Jerry Falwell in order to maintain his viability as a presidential candidate. Goldwater didn't shout when angry or irritated (as does McCain), but the old maverick didn't have to raise his voice to make his feelings known when a matter of principle was involved. Time and again during his 1964 race for the White House Goldwater turned down advice that he change his position on issues that were bringing his poll numbers down, telling campaign strategists that he'd rather lose the election than represent himself as "something I'm not."

---

primary. Both Bush and McCain, though pushed by civil rights organizations and the media to speak out, maintained an expedient silence on the issue. Only when the primary was over and the campaign had moved on to Michigan and other northern primaries did McCain discover the error of his ways, telling reporters aboard his Straight Talk (*sic*) Express that, come to think of it, he was *against* South Carolina's flying the Confederate flag all along.

A prime example was his insistence on addressing the issue of nuclear weapons strategy in the Cold War, even after his staff pointed out that his very use of the word "nuclear" set off alarm bells in voters' minds. Barry's response was that he hadn't entered the presidential race in order to stand silent on what he thought was the most critical issue facing the American people.

The problem from a political standpoint was that Goldwater, as a brigadier general in the Air Force reserve and ranking Republican member of the Senate Armed Services Committee, let his expertise on nuclear weaponry cloud his judgment as to what the lay citizen could understand; not to mention the headline hounds of the Washington news media, always quick to oversimplify and sensationalize a complex political subject.

Since the beginning of the North Atlantic Treaty Organization in the early years of the Cold War, questions had been raised in the Pentagon about command authority regarding the use of nuclear weapons. Though it was obvious that only the president could order the use of strategic nuclear bombs, arguments were made, pro and con, about whether the use of tactical nukes could be ordered by the commander of NATO in the event of a Soviet attack on Western Europe.

Goldwater, asked his opinion, came out publicly in favor of giving the NATO chief that authority; but the Associated Press, making no distinctions, reported his position in terms of giving "commanders in the field" (i.e., anyone from a Corps commander to a regimental colonel), the power to push the nuclear button.

It was a distortion of what Goldwater had actually said, but the image of Barry the nuclear war hawk was seized on and embellished by his opponents' TV admen in both the Republican primaries and the general election. The more he tried to clarify his stand, the worse the problem became, especially after Bill Moyers, the Karl Rove of Lyndon Johnson's campaign staff, gave the go-ahead for two TV spots showing mushroom clouds obliterating little girls, one eating an ice cream cone, the second blowing daisy petals—showing what could happen, in short, if Barry Goldwater were elected president. (See Chapter 7 for Goldwater's personal reaction to the ads.)

What particularly galled members of Goldwater's staff was the fact that at the very time these TV spots were being prepared, Johnson invited Barry to the White House to propose they both agree not to use either foreign policy or civil rights as a campaign issue. As Goldwater later told friends, he was angered by LBJ's duplicity but not surprised. He'd known Johnson to be "a lying sonofabitch" since their days together in the Senate and nothing the man said or did as president—including his use of a sham incident in the Tonkin Gulf to step up U.S. involvement in the Vietnam War—had changed his opinion.

After objections were filed with the Democratic National Committee, the mushroom cloud ads were pulled. They had run only one time, but as Moyers later told Johnson biographer Merle Miller, one showing had been enough to brand Barry Goldwater, Texas-style, as a nuclear monster. Still, despite the fact that every mention of nuclear defense policy reminded listeners of the ads, Barry wouldn't stop addressing the issue.

It was a matter of principle.

* * *

Goldwater's political credo on controversial issues, as Lee Edwards pointed out in his 1995 biography of the senator, was Edmund Burke's counsel that "Your representative owes you his judgment as well as his industry. He betrays your best interest if he sacrifices his judgment to your opinion." That Goldwater would carry the same credo into a campaign for the White House is what separated him from John McCain and others whose pursuit of the presidency leads them, both literally and figuratively, down the road to Lynchburg, Virginia.

But McCain's kiss-up to Jerry Falwell aside, there are issues that he does indeed stand rock-solid on: campaign finance "reform" for one, but most notably, his unwavering support for the Bush-Cheney administration's reckless commitment of American lives to an open-ended war of choice under a smokescreen of lies and deceit not unlike that used by Lyndon Johnson in pushing the fraudulent Tonkin Gulf resolution through Congress in 1964; which leads us to the second good reason I don't see John McCain—despite the rave reviews he gets from a fawning Washington press corps—in the image of his Arizona predecessor, Barry Goldwater.

Both Goldwater and McCain shared the experience of having served the country in combat, but Goldwater came away with a far different view regarding the use of American force overseas. The Goldwater Doctrine: *There are wars with limited objectives but there is no such thing as a "limited" war.* ("Either win the war in a short time...or pull out all our troops and come home.") Unlike McCain, whose "exit" strategy in Iraq involves a "surge" in troop strength in what Donald Rumsfeld called "a long, hard slog," Goldwater drew the line on any protracted war that brought an ever-increasing number of fighting men into battle without a clear, foreseeable objective.

Nor did Goldwater, unlike McCain and his fellow Neo-Cons in the Bush Cheney administration, take the Wilsonian view that it was America's mission from God to spread democracy throughout the world. Despite the simplistic label pinned on him by political opponents and the press at the time, Barry was a foreign policy realist with a studied understanding of the complexity of the world around us and the limits of American power. Years later, after reviewing the history of U.S. involvement in Vietnam, he would write, "Vietnam is about halfway around the world from Washington. It's as large as the major European nations, with nearly 130,000 square miles...Its ancient recorded history goes back to 111 B.C....We entered (that country) with considerable ignorance."

Increase the square mileage to 170,000, add two millennia to the history, reiterate with emphasis that line about "considerable ignorance"—then add to all that the same scorching critique of the Bush-Cheney administration's planning and conduct of the Iraq war that he made of the Johnson-McNamara conduct of the Vietnam War forty years ago—and you have the opening salvo of a Barry Goldwater presidential debate with either John McCain or Hillary Clinton.

* * *

"I admired Truman. We didn't agree on much but he was a patriot and straight-talker. You always knew where he stood. That's rare in a politician."

—BARRY GOLDWATER IN A LETTER TO THE AUTHOR, FEBRUARY 1974

What If?

I've been hooked on alternative history, serious or otherwise, ever since *Look* magazine devoted an issue to a fiction titled, "If the South had won the Civil War." That was in the early 1950s, not long after James Thurber, with a lighter take on the same theme, came up with "If Grant had been Drunk at Appomattox."

For the student of political history (serious or otherwise), the alternative genre has two bracing appeals: first, it stretches the mind, an exercise especially recommended for anyone past the ossified age of sixty; second, it has the benefit of taking you away, if only temporarily, from the dreary contemplation of what American voters in 2008 actually have to choose from in the way of presidential candidates.

Imagining "what if" Barry Goldwater were running for president in 2008 isn't that big a stretch when you consider that even *in* his time he was said to be *out* of his time. (He didn't mind that being said of him, either.

When Vice President Hubert Humphrey quipped that "Goldwater has one of the finest minds of the century—the 14th century," Barry not only laughed but quoted it in his speeches as well.)

The quality that endeared Goldwater to his followers, after all, had as much to do with *how* as *where* he stood on the issues. When twenty years after his retirement from the Senate a Pete Hamill could write that "in spite of my own continuing (though chastened) liberal faith, I miss Barry Goldwater," be assured it wasn't because he'd come to share Barry's views on Social Security or the defense budget.

No, what's most missed about Barry Goldwater—not only by Hamill but also by the Republican party and the country as a whole—is the quality he admired in Harry Truman: "You always knew where he stood. That's rare in a politician."

And more: Goldwater, to these biased eyes, brought an element to the politics of his time even more rare in a politician known for his deep-rooted political convictions: "Politics wouldn't be politics without a fight," he wrote. "However, I've always said that to disagree you don't have to be disagreeable. My mother taught me that, and so did [my uncle] Morris."[3]

---

[3] Goldwater frequently spoke of the influence his uncle Morris had in shaping his political character and outlook. Morris Goldwater, older brother of Barry's father Baron, was the first member of the family to enter politics, serving ten terms as mayor of Prescott, Arizona, back during the days when the state (then a territory) was best known for the Gunfight at the OK Corral. Described by Barry as "a stalwart in the Democratic party," Morris Goldwater's ability to rise above partisanship and maintain close personal friendships with political adversaries left an abiding impression on his young nephew (*The Goldwaters of Arizona*, a 1986 history/biography by Dean Smith).

Civility in Political Discourse

A Barry Goldwater running for president in 2008 would have no problem repeating words George W. Bush uttered in January 2001: "America at its best matches a commitment to principle with a concern for civility. Civility is not a tactic or a sentiment. It is a determined choice of trust over cynicism, of community over chaos."

It was one of the two great rhetorical frauds in Dubya's soaring Inaugural Address (the other, that in our international dealings "we will show purpose without arrogance"). But in Goldwater's case, the words would carry the imprint of a national leader who saw politics itself as a match of principle and civility. A Karl Rove wouldn't have lasted a day in a Barry Goldwater campaign, much less a Barry Goldwater White House.

An incident comes to mind from the 1964 presidential campaign: When a high-level member of Lyndon Johnson's White House staff was arrested on a morals charge in a downtown Washington men's room, word immediately went out that no member of the Goldwater staff was to respond to questions about the incident from inquiring reporters. Though public morality was at the top of the campaign's agenda, private morality (unless it compromised national security) was off-limits. Throughout his political career, Goldwater held to a libertarian code that separated public and private affairs in the political arena.

The best-known example of Barry's ability to disagree without being disagreeable—to enjoy the company of a fellow politician of widely variant views—was his ongoing friendship with John F. Kennedy. Both men, the

Conservative from the Southwest and the Liberal from the Northeast, had come to the U.S. Senate as freshman members in January 1953. Their friendship, as Goldwater makes clear in his memoir, was genuine, transcending the bitter partisan debates that took place in the Senate during the McCarthy years.

"There were four relationships in Congress that meant a great deal to me," Goldwater would write after he retired, "the Kennedys (Jack and Ted), Senator Paul Laxalt, and the two Arizona congressmen, Mo Udall and John Rhodes. With the Kennedys, patriotism drew us together. [They] returned the compliment. Ted expressed their view to a friend of mine: 'I think my brother Jack liked Barry Goldwater so much because Barry was so good at poking fun at himself. I believe everybody in Washington likes Barry today because he came out of the 1964 loss with grace and humor.'"

Try matching those words—"grace and humor"—to any of the piranha ideologues operating under "Conservative Republican" colors in George W. Bush's compassionate Washington, a town where deviation from the Bush-Cheney line can get a paraplegic Vietnam veteran tarred as a fifth-column accomplice of Osama bin Laden.

* * *

"Our Constitution seeks to allow freedom for everyone, not merely those professing certain moral or religious views of ultimate right. We don't have to look back centuries to see such dangers. Look at the carnage in the name of religious

righteousness in Iran. The long and bloody division of Northern Ireland. The Christian-Moslem and Moslem-Moslem 'holy war' in Lebanon."

—BARRY GOLDWATER (1988), FOLLOWING HIS RETIREMENT FROM THE

UNITED STATES SENATE

Civility In, Religiosity Out

Second only to bringing civility back to the White House, a Goldwater candidacy would make the case for showing Elmer Gantry the door. The Bush-nurtured program of "faith-based initiatives" has never been anything more than a Great Society giveaway in clerical drag, another Rovean ploy using taxpayer money to shore up support among Bush's evangelical base. Under a Goldwater administration, that spigot would be shut off, the principle of separation of church and politics reaffirmed by a president so retro he's repelled by the Clinton/Bush practice of church-hopping on Sunday.

Like George H. W. Bush, Barry came from a political generation that flaunted neither war records nor religious faith. I never heard either man speak of his World War II experience unless pressed, and religion in the early years of both men's political careers was considered (except in the case of John F. Kennedy in 1960) a private matter. In *The Conscience of a Conservative,* however—the 1960 manifesto that confirmed his arrival as a major figure on the national scene—Goldwater wrote openly of his principles being "derived from the nature of man and from the truths that God has revealed about His creation."

216

"The basic difference between conservatives and liberals," he wrote, "is that conservatives account for the whole man while liberals tend to stress the material man. Conservatism puts material things in their proper place, subsidiary to the spiritual side of man's nature."[4]

Four years later, as the presidential nominee of his party, Barry would reflect the same theme in his acceptance speech at the Republican national convention, sounding like nothing so much as, in the words of Theodore H. White (*The Making of the President 1964*), "the Prophet Goldwater" who "insists that man must be good, that it is their moral duty to be good." Yet, for all his thunderous moralizing, sincere though it was, the Prophet with a libertarian streak would later write, "I am concerned about clergy engaged in a heavy-handed, continuing attempt to use political means to obtain moral ends—and vice-versa. It is one of the most dangerous trends in this country."

$$\star \quad \star \quad \star$$

White House tradition has it that every president graces the Roosevelt room where the Cabinet meets with a portrait of his favorite predecessor: for Bill Clinton it was Andrew Jackson; for George W. Bush it's Teddy Roosevelt. One guess whose portrait would have been on the wall if Barry Goldwater had become president? No, not Calvin

---

[4] An important distinction here: Though a champion of free-market economics and individual entrepreneurship, Goldwater never viewed material success as the core value in a free society; this, contrary to an especially fatuous (even for him) column by the *New York Times* Neo-Conservative David Brooks in October 2006, wherein Brooks portrayed Barry's emphasis on individualism in terms of economic atavism.

Coolidge. Much as Barry admired him, Silent Cal wasn't his favorite (he was, however, Ronald Reagan's). My own guess, up until February 1974, would have been either Herbert Hoover (a fellow Westerner and to hell with what the Liberals thought) or "Bull Moose" Roosevelt.

But that was the month I read a news story out of Phoenix that quoted Barry as having called Harry Truman "possibly the best president of this century." *Harry Truman*? Fair Deal Harry, the Democrat's Democrat? Puzzled, I wrote a column about it in the old *Washington Star*, raising the question as to whether my old boss was undergoing some sort of political transformation or had simply been misquoted. A few days later I received the following reply:

February 20, 1974

Dear Vic:

In your column the other evening you expressed wonderment at how I could rate Harry Truman as possibly the best president of this century. I have to tell you that others around the United States have expressed a similar puzzlement, but I must add immediately that an overwhelming number of people where I have said this, even amongst gatherings of Republicans and conservatives have cheered my remarks. The latter, however, is beside the point.

The first question is of the order, and I hope I can answer it in a very short fashion. Think back over all the presidents we've had and try to think what any one of them did in his term of office or terms of office that he specifically is remembered for.

Oh, we might come up with Washington as the founder of the country, with Jefferson for the words he wrote before he was president in the Declaration of Independence, Monroe for the doctrine he had nothing to do with but which carries his name, and then we come to Lincoln who was above everything else a leader. Then we start through another long period of presidents who did nothing remarkable during their tenure of office, and we come to Teddy Roosevelt. Well, we might say Teddy built the Panama Canal, and so he did, and he led the charge up San Juan Hill in Cuba, and his name is attached to most of all of the important developments in my state, but that still doesn't get to the point.

We then go through the subsequent presidents and come to Truman, and now is where I attempt to make my point. What the presidents we remember are remembered for has been leadership in times of peril. Washington led us in the peril of birth; Jefferson led us in the peril of an emerging government; skip Monroe; we come to Lincoln who guided us through the most desperate times in our history; then Teddy who did the same thing; and that brings us up to Truman.

I didn't agree with much that Truman did when he was doing what he was doing, but one thing I could always say: I knew where he stood and I didn't have to wait around for a press conference, a television show, or a group of press agents to tell me what it was he said or what he was supposed to have said.

In other words, he was always out in front and now that I look back on it, this is the thing that we've needed ever since Truman, and we need it today probably more than any time in our history.

I'll never forget a lecture I attended of General George Patton's one night when he was making critiques of the maneuvers of the day and he held up a plate on which was a wet noodle. He attempted to push this noodle across the plate. It couldn't be done, so he pulled it. And he said, "Gentlemen, you don't push the noodle; you pull it." In other words, you lead it.

If you haven't gotten my point up to now, Vic, call me. I'll buy you a short hooker and we can go into it in more depth.

With best wishes and admiration for the good you're doing,
Barry

Leadership, yes, "always out in front." But rereading that letter it occurred to me that, unmentioned in his praise of Harry Truman, was the fact that, for all their differences in political philosophy, Barry and Harry shared the reputation of being not simply straight-talkers but, even rarer among those who survive in Washington for any length of time, incorruptibles.

Truman, though a product of the Pendergast machine in Kansas City, made his national reputation—and earned the Democratic vice presidential nomination in 1944—on the strength of his impartial, let-the-chips-fall-where-they-may Senate investigation of war profiteering. Whatever was said of the small men around him, no one ever questioned the moral integrity of the Man from Independence.

So, too, his Republican admirer, Barry Goldwater. For Barry, conservative values in a public official began not with a laundry list of public issues but personal probity: "Lobbyists have money," he would say. "I always tell them the same thing: If they want to contribute to my campaign, fine. But if they give me campaign funds with the idea that I'll vote their way, they can get the hell out of my office."

Lobbyist-paid junkets to play golf at St. Andrews, pork-barrel "earmarks" by the thousands, bridges to nowhere, congressional wives and family members hired by corporate lobbyists, multi-billion-dollar no-bid government contracts to privileged conglomerates with White House connections—oh, yes, Pete Hamill, what the country needs today is a Barry Goldwater raising hell. But not as a presidential candidate in the 2008 election. No, that's too much to hope for. Who'd nominate him? Certainly not George W. Bush's Republican party.

Chapter 14

THE GREAT DIVIDE

"The great danger in the new conservative movement is that instead of broadening its base, the movement might tear itself and the GOP apart."

—Barry Goldwater, 1988

THERE'LL BE CANDIDATES running under the Republican label when you go to the polls November 4, 2008, but don't be fooled. If the truth-in-labeling law applied to politicians, they'd all be operating under cease-and-desist orders from the Federal Trade Commission.

How did Will Rogers put it when asked about his party affiliation back in the 1930s? "I belong to no organized political party. I'm a Democrat."

Updated for members of the onetime party of Lincoln as we head toward the 2008 presidential election, the line should read, "I belong to no recognizable political party.

I'm a Republican"; which brings us to Nebraska's maverick Senator Chuck Hagel's openly wondering in 2005 "whether I'm in the same party I started out in." That, from a man said to be entertaining ideas of running for the Republican presidential nomination in 2008.

Two pieces of news, Chuck, both bad: First, the answer to your question is no, neither you nor any Republican who voted for George W. Bush in the year 2000 are members of the party we knew seven years ago (which accounts for why millions, like this writer, abandoned the party's candidates in 2006); second, the very fact that you have the intellectual honesty to ask that question automatically disqualifies you as a serious contender for a Republican presidential nomination in 2008 or any time in the foreseeable future.

But don't take it too hard. You're in the best of company. Barry Goldwater, were he alive, would have the same problem, as would every 20th-century Republican leader not imbued with what traditional conservative scholar Jeffrey Hart puts down as George W. Bush's "tendency to privilege ideology over realism."

"George W. Bush represents a huge swing away from...traditional conservative Republicanism," wrote Hart in the *American Conservative* shortly before the midterm congressional elections of 2006. "But the conservative movement in America has followed him, evacuating prudence and realism for ideology and folly. Left behind has been the experienced realism of James Burnham. Also vacated, the Burkean realism of Willmoore Kendall...the individualism of Frank Meyer and the commonsense libertarianism of Barry Goldwater."

Add to these virtues the innate decency of Ronald Reagan and the informed civility of George H. W. Bush, conservative values not simply evacuated but mutilated by what Hart aptly describes as "the moral authoritarianism" of the Bush-Cheney administration. (I'd be tempted to call George W.'s moralism "Cromwellian" but for the fact that Cromwell, for all his warts, wasn't hypocrite enough to call himself a "compassionate Roundhead.")

Which leads to the real question Chuck Hagel and like-minded Republicans should be asking as we scan the littered political landscape left by the midterm elections of 2006 and look ahead to 2008: After nearly a decade of Neo/Theo Conservative hegemony over what was once our political home, is the Republican party we once knew salvageable? Or to put it more bluntly (the way Barry Goldwater might), after eight years of George W. Bush and Richard B. Cheney in the White House, is there anything left of the party of Lincoln worth saving?

The Future of the Republican Party

When Abraham Lincoln said a house divided against itself cannot stand, he obviously wasn't thinking about America's two major political parties. Division, sometimes bitter, has been the rule rather than the exception in Republican and Democratic history alike, whether it be East Coast versus

225

Heartland Republicans, Northern versus Southern Democrats, tariff boosters against free traders, isolationists against globalists.

Example: "Sometimes I think we'd be better off if we just sawed off the Eastern seaboard and let it float out into the Atlantic."

Remember that line? You should if you were around in the 1960s and follow Republican politics. It was Barry Goldwater's off-the-hip solution to the division then existing between Heartland and East Coast Republicans. Yet, when the moment came to break ranks in 1960, it was Goldwater who held the party together when Right-wingers threatened to bolt at the Chicago convention that year: "We are conservatives," Barry told his followers. "This great Republican party is our historical house. This is our home. Now some of us don't agree with every statement in the official platform of our party, but I might remind you that this is always true in every platform of an American political party."

That was the Goldwater I knew, a student of political history who, for all his refusal to bend on matters of bedrock principle, would in the years following his retirement from the Senate write, "For a democracy to function, there has to be give and take, some room for compromise."

A political prophet as well, who, seeing the direction his party was headed in the mid-1990s, would warn, "The GOP will be weakened if it adopts the exclusionary views of the Religious Right."

Political analysts saw the outcome of the 2006 midterm elections as a massive repudiation of the Bush-Cheney "stay-the-course" policy in Iraq and the culture of corruption induced by a self-aggrandizing Republican Congress. But a history-minded Barry Goldwater might read deeper significance into returns that showed even GOP candidates not tarred by those issues—moderates like Senator Lincoln Chafee of Rhode Island and Congressman Jim Leach of Iowa—were also swept away in what was as much an anti-Republican as Democratic landslide.

What Chafee and Leach were tarred with, their independence from the White House notwithstanding, was the image of the Nation's business at a standstill while the Religious Right, in pursuit of its "Right to Life" agenda, turned a private family tragedy into a political farce.[1]

The Terri Schiavo case would be in 2005 what the Gingrich shutdown of the federal government, that led to the reelection of Bill Clinton, had been ten years earlier: public notice—as if any were needed—that the "great" Republican party Barry Goldwater spoke of had been taken over by zealous ideologues and exclusionary Theocrats.

Unfortunately for today's Republican National Committee, the next time a threatened party split occurs, there'll be no Barry Goldwater around to remind the

---

[1] A special word here for one of the worst losses suffered by the Republican party in 2006, that of Colorado Congressman Joel Hefley, a traditional Goldwater-style conservative who, seeing the radical Right direction his party was headed and outraged by the corruption around him in the Hastert-DeLay-led House, retired from Congress. It was Hefley, as a member of the House Ethics Committee, who cast the sole Republican vote to investigate charges of campaign finance corruption against Tom DeLay—an act of non-partisan principle for which he paid the price by being removed from the Committee by Speaker Hastert.

feuding factions that "This is our house"; though even if there were, it's doubtful his plea for party unity would do any good. The divide in the Neo-Theo-Con-dominated Republican party nurtured by the Bush-Cheney White House, like the divide that brought down the house of Whigs in the 1850s, is too great to be breached.

Compromise?

You won't find the word in the political lexicon of the Religious Right, nor is there any way for a great national party or leader to meet the demands of the Terri Schiavo fanatics without sooner or later self-destructing. Has the Scripture-quoting, born-again leadership of George W. Bush been all a True Believer could ask for in an American president? You'd think so, but in an op-ed diatribe written for the *New York Times* two days after the midterm election of 2006, David Kuo, one-time deputy director of George W.'s Office of Faith-Based Initiatives, had this to say:

"Conservative Christians (like me) were promised that having an evangelical like Mr. Bush in the White House was a dream come true. Well, it wasn't. Not by a long shot. The administration accomplished little that evangelicals really cared about.

"Nowhere was this clearer than on the issue of abortion. Despite strong Republican majorities and his own pro-life stands, Mr. Bush settled for the largely symbolic partial-birth abortion restriction rather than pursuing more substantial change...Evangelicals are not likely to fall for such promises in the future."

Oh, that this were true and that Karl Rove's beloved evangelical base were to do what one of its lay leaders, Paul Weyrich, professed to do several years back and renounce mundane politics because it hadn't, at that moment in time, given him everything he wanted (one of the vicissitudes of the democratic process that true-believing Theocrats would, if they could, do away with).

But no, don't believe for a moment that, whatever mid-level evangelical drones like David Kuo do, Religious Right leaders like Pat Robertson, Jerry Falwell, and James Dobson are going to give up their "dream come true" of controlling the agenda of one of America's two major political parties and virtually dictating who that party's presidential and vice presidential nominees will be: John McCain making his pilgrimage to Lynchburg; Mitt Romney, a candidate who in another era might be addressing serious issues but instead blathering like an Elmer Gantry congregant about the threat same-sex marriage poses to the future of Western civilization; even that old cosmopolite Rudy Giuliani, hallucinating that a multiple divorcé who roomed with gay friends could win a Republican nomination, hustling south to speak on behalf of Pat Robertson's protégé, Ralph Reed, in Reed's unsuccessful campaign for lieutenant governor of Georgia.

So much for what happens to the leadership of one of America's two major political parties when it expands its base at the expense of its purpose; not to mention, in the case of the Neo-Con invaders who seized the Republican foreign policy agenda in 2001, its principles: The party house stands but it's no longer recognizable as the home we knew in the days when national leaders like Barry Goldwater and Ronald Reagan were defining its conservative agenda.

To repeat the questions then: Is the Republican party we once knew salvageable and, given the damage done by the Bush-Cheney White House and DeLay-Hastert Congress in the past half-decade, is there anything left of it worth saving?

Let me, contrary to my own cynical nature, put on Barry's optimist hat and answer "Yes" in both cases—but with a cynic's caveat. The salvage can only come if the patient here dies and is reborn; which is to say, the transmogrified political entity now passing itself off as the party of Lincoln will have to pay the price for its masquerade, as occurred in November 2006—and, given the in-denial response to that election by the party's leaders, will likely recur in 2008.

Do Hillary Clinton's Democrats of today have anything better in the way of a vision of America's future than did Lyndon Johnson's Democrats four decades ago? No, but the lesson of 2006 for traditional Republicans with an eye to reclaiming their party was that political campaigns waged with a Manichean view of that future (Karl Rove directing, Ann Coulter writing the script) don't sit well with an American electorate traditionally repelled by ideological zealots of either Left or Right.

Nothing, in short, can cleanse the political palate better than a few bitter pills swallowed in losing elections; after which, their perks of power taken away, the Jerry Falwells now inhabiting the house of Lincoln might be persuaded to pick up their psalm books and move to their real political home, the Prohibition Party, while their Neo-

Con allies, done in by the Axis of Evil, slouch back to the think tank cubicles from whence they came.

Die and Be Reborn

An option to think about for those Republicans who, like Chuck Hagel (and this writer), no longer recognize the party they started out in, and would, if they could, bring back to the ballot:

- A Republican party that renders unto Caesar and unto God, but on separate days of the week.

- A Republican party that sees America as a beacon, not the policeman for the world.

- A Republican party wedded to the economic realism of Milton Friedman and Herb Stein, not the irresponsible debt-and-deficit economics of Arthur Laffer and Robert Mundell.

- A Republican party that sees family values as something for the family, not the state, to define.

- A Republican party alert to the danger of "a robust executive authority" and of those who, in the name of saving freedom, would destroy it.

- A Republican leadership that sees power in a free society the way Barry Goldwater saw it, not as an end in itself, but as the means to an end.

* * *

On the wall above my desk, to the right of a Leroy Neiman of another great American authentic, Paul "Bear" Bryant, is my favorite memento from a half-dozen national campaigns: a print of the Norman Rockwell charcoal of Barry Goldwater that appeared on the cover of the *Saturday Evening Post* shortly after he won the Republican presidential nomination in July 1964. And above the print, these words from his acceptance speech:

> *The Good Lord raised up this mighty republic to be a home for the brave and to flourish as the land of the free. We must reaffirm the great truths that have given life and strength to America. We must set the tides running again in the cause of freedom.*

Half a dozen campaigns from the '60s to the '90s, and wouldn't you know, the campaign I'm proudest of is the one in which my candidate wasn't simply beaten but lost by what at the time was the biggest landslide in American presidential history.

What's more, it was a loss we knew was coming from the day the campaign began. How could we not? We had a candidate who in his very first pitch for support at the national convention said in effect, *This is what I stand for. If you like what I have to say, welcome aboard. If not, don't expect me to spin my position, kiss your baby, or be something I'm not, to get your vote.* ("Anyone who joins us in all sincerity, we welcome," were Goldwater's exact words. "Those who do not care for our cause, we don't expect to enter our ranks in any case.")

Believe me, it was a presidential campaign unlike any run before or since. An inner-city catchphrase, "Tell it like it is," had taken hold, and here America had a presidential candidate for a major political party doing just that, no gloss or varnish. Another phrase of the time, popularized by comedian Flip Wilson, was "What you see is what you get," and nobody who saw Barry Goldwater during those hectic eight campaign weeks ever doubted for a moment that he was the same man in the public arena that he was away from the cameras and the kliegs.

After a week on the Goldwater press plane, the *New Yorker*'s Richard Rovere, never having seen a candidate like Barry in two decades of covering politics, told his readers it wasn't so much a campaign he was covering as a "caper." Bob Novak, in a similar vein, told followers of his syndicated column that Barry was "writing the book on how not to run for president."

At campaign headquarters at the Camelback Inn at Scottsdale, Arizona, election night, the landslide was being reported by the networks before the sun went down, with people in Arizona and other Western states still lined up to vote. Not that it would have made any real difference if the networks had held back: When you lose the presidency by thirteen million votes, as Barry later said, the only thing left for you to do is "sit on your porch and whistle 'Hail to the Chief.'" As the night wore on, he had only one concern—that whatever the tally, he carry his home state. (He did; Arizona was one of the five states that went his way.)

The next morning, after a standard concession speech, Barry Goldwater, as reported by *Newsweek* correspondent William Tuohy, "philosophized about his defeat":

> *Goldwater:* "I'll live with it. I'll keep on kicking and living and talking and planting cactus and playing golf—and working in politics."

True to his promise, four years later, the old maverick was back in the United States Senate, speaking the truth, "disturbing the public peace," blowing the whistle on the "lies and evasions" that characterized the Vietnam/Watergate years, as unrelenting in his criticism of a Republican White House as he had been of Lyndon Johnson. (When the time came for Republicans to deliver the bad news to Richard Nixon after the Watergate scandal reached critical mass, Goldwater was one of the three members of the congressional delegation sent to the White House to tell Nixon if he didn't resign he'd be impeached.)

Sui generis, even in death

At Barry Goldwater's funeral in Phoenix in June 1998, not one but three religions were on hand to deliver eulogies: An Episcopalian minister of his own faith, a rabbi representing his grandfather's, and a Navajo chief in full regalia come to chant last respects to the "blood brother" his tribesmen called "Chischilly" (the curly-haired one). Though their words were different, their message was the same: The man is gone, but his spirit remains.

Indeed it does, and not just for those who knew and

were touched by Barry Goldwater in life. Ahead of his time in some ways, contrarily behind the times in others, his example is timeless in those matters of character and courage—in his passion for freedom and love not simply of country but his countrymen.

"I miss Barry Goldwater," wrote liberal Pete Hamill in the summer of 2004. "More than ever." You're not alone, Pete. So does his party. Even more so his country.

INDEX

9/11
  Bush, George W., 73, 132, 183
  Cheney, Dick, 80–81
  Coulter, Ann, 123
  Iraq War (2003–), 124
  midterm elections (2002), 124
  Neo-Cons and, 101, 104, 110
  Ponnuru, Ramesh, 145
  Rove, Karl, 124
  Snow, Tony, 115–16
  Yoo, John, 198–99
  See also State of the Union
    address (2002); Terrorism
80th Congress, 12, 48
104th Congress, 35–36
  Armey, Dick, 36, 48
  Clinton, William Jefferson,
    12–13, 41, 48, 52–53
  Contract with America,
    36–37, 40, 49
  Goldwater, Barry, 10, 11
  government shutdown, 45,
    46–47, 227
  Kasich, John, 36, 47, 48
  Medicare, 45–46
  Paxon, Bill, 36
  Theo-Cons and, 48–50
  Walker, Bob, 36
  See also DeLay, Tom; Gingrich,
    Newt;
105th Congress, 52–53

A
ABC (television network), 120, 121,
  131
Abortion
  Bush, George W., 228
  Clinton, Hillary, 143
  Contract with America, 49
  Deaver, Mike, 24
  electoral campaigns and, 29–30
  Falwell, Jerry, 25
  family planning and, 50
  family values and, 50
  Keyes, Alan, 140, 141, 144
  Kuo, David, 228
  O'Connor, Sandra Day, 206
  Republican conventions, 21, 22

Roe v. Wade, 27–28, 29,
  143–44
  social conservatism and, 23
Abramoff, Jack, 155, 161,
  163–64, 165, 166–69, 171
Abu Ghraib, 186
Acheson, Dean, 106
Addington, David, 96
Advertising, political, 133–35,
  137, 209
AFL-CIO, 26
Agnew, Spiro, 83–84, 118–21,
  122, 126, 127
AIDS, 50
Ailes, Roger, 127, 129–30, 131
Air Force One, 47, 55, 74, 80,
  81, 96, 186
Albright, Madeleine, 100
Allen, O. K., 116
All the King's Men (Warren), 192
al Qaeda, 80, 81, 101, 113
American Conservative (magazine),
  194
American Psychiatric Association,
  136
Anderson, William, 151
Antiabortion movement. *See*
  Abortion
Arctic National Wildlife Refuge,
  173
Armey, Dick, 36, 48
Armitage, Laura, 99
Armitage, Richard, 99, 100, 104
Ashcroft, John
  Attorney General, 160,
    173–74, 203–4
  lobbying, 158, 159, 160, 173–74
  Starr, Kenneth, 53
  states' rights, 203–4
  U.S. Senate race (2000),
    155–58, 160
  Yoo, John, 198
Associated Press (AP), 94, 120, 208
Attorney General. *See* Ashcroft,
  John; Gonzalez, Alberto
Austin, Warren, 106
Axis of Evil, 114, 115

B
Babbitt (Lewis), 192
Baker, Howard, 68, 158
Baker, James A., III, 68, 90
Balanced budget, 36
Barbour, Haley, 45, 46
Barnes, Fred, 123
Bauer, Gary, 139, 142, 143, 145,
  150–51, 181
Begala, Paul, 127
Bennett, Bill, 6
Berger, Sandy, 110
Bierce, Ambrose, 49
bin Laden, Osama, 59, 61, 110,
  116, 122
Bloggers, 126, 127
Blumenthal, Sidney, 182
Bob Jones University, 26
Bodham, Samuel, 187
Body Politic, The (Gold and
  Cheney), 83–84
Boehner, John, 132
Bolten, Josh, 59, 77
Bork, Robert, 199, 203, 204
Brandeis, Louis, 191
Brave New World (Huxley), 148
Brinkley, David, 135
Brooks, David, 123, 217
*Brown v. Topeka Board of
  Education,* 28, 29
Brown, Michael, 184, 185
Brown, Ron, 183
Bryan, William Jennings, 48, 153
Buckley, William F., 13, 126–27,
  194
Burch, Dean, 14
Burke, Edmund, 210
Burnham, James, 224
Bush, Barbara, 57, 65, 71, 75–76
Bush, George H. W.
  Ailes, Roger, 129
  Bush, George W., 55, 57,
    58–59, 64–67, 70, 71,
    75–76, 89–90, 115, 116
  Bush, Jeb, 57, 70, 71–72, 75–76
  Cheney, Dick, 62, 63, 64–65,
    82, 90–91, 96, 116
  Iran-Contra scandal, 51–52

Iraq War (1991), 90–91, 102, 104–5, 115, 116
Iraq War (2003–), 115–16
Neo-Cons and, 62, 63, 64
partisanship, 55–56
political career, 67–70
political discourse, 216, 225
Powell, Colin, 62, 91, 104–5
presidential leadership, 72–73, 74–75
Rather, Dan, 129–30
Religious Right, 21–22, 26, 27, 32
Republican national convention (1980), 18, 19
Rice, Condoleezza, 99
Rumsfeld, Donald, 77, 87–89, 92, 115
Snow, Tony, 115–16
symbolism and, 183
Bush, George W.
  Abramoff, Jack, 161
  Abu Ghraib, 186
  accountability, 185–86
  Air Force One, 74, 80, 96, 186
  Ashcroft, John, 158
  Bush, George H. W., 55, 57, 58–59, 64–67, 70, 71, 75–76, 89–90, 115, 116
  character of, 96–97
  Cheney, Dick, 60, 61, 64–65, 81, 82, 84
  conservatism and, 4, 5, 224, 225
  corruption, 161, 162, 166, 167, 168, 170, 171, 172–73
  cultural policy, 4–5
  domestic policy, 4
  election of 1994, 2
  election of 2000, 2
  executive power, 193, 194, 195, 196–97, 200
  faith-based community, 22
  foreign policy, 100, 101
  Hurricane Katrina, 184–88
  Hussein, Saddam, 90, 116
  Intelligent Design, 152–53
  Iraq War, 211

McCain, John, 206, 207, 210
media and, 122, 123, 124, 128
national security, 5
nation building, 38
oil industry, 172–73
partisanship, 132–33
political discourse, 214, 215, 216
Powell, Colin, 105, 107
presidential campaigning, 57–58
presidential campaign team (2000), 63–64
presidential leadership, 72, 73–74
presidential personnel decisions, 56
religious conservatism, 33
Religious Right and, 26, 228
Republican national convention (1980), 17–18
Republican Party, 230
Rice, Condoleezza, 107–8, 109
Rumsfeld, Donald, 59–60, 76, 89, 92–94
Snow, Tony, 132
State of the Union address (2002), 81, 100, 111–15, 132
stem cell research, 145–48
Supreme Court nominations, 143
symbolism, 183–88
WMDs, 109, 114
Bush, Jeb, 18, 57, 70–72, 75–76, 152
Bush, Laura, 77
Bush, Marvin, 57
Bush, Prescott, 21
Bush, Robin, 65

C
Campaign ads, 133–35, 137, 209
Campaign finance reform, 44, 210
Cannon, Lou, 24–25
Card, Andy, 56–57, 59, 63

Carnahan, Jean, 157
Carnahan, Mel, 156
Carter, Jimmy, 6–7, 27, 29, 96, 182
Carville, James, 41, 127
Cassel, Douglas, 197–98
Casserly, Jack, 133
Catholicism, 48–49
CBS (television network), 119, 120, 121, 129–30, 136
Central Intelligence Agency (CIA)
  Bush, George H. W., 66, 68, 88, 89, 92, 129
  Cheney, Dick, 105
  Hussein, Saddam, 110
  Powell, Colin, 106
  Tenet, George, 105
  Torture Memo, 170–71
Chafee, Lincoln, 226
Chalabi, Ahmed, 105, 195
Chamberlain, Neville, 124
Checkbook clergy, 31, 33, 206
Chemical industry, 171
Cheney, Dick, 60–64
  9/11, 80–81
  Abu Ghraib, 186
  Air Force One, 80, 81
  Bush, George H. W., 59, 62, 63, 64–65, 82, 90–91, 96, 116
  Bush, George W., 60, 61, 64–65, 66, 81, 82, 84
  conservatism and, 4, 5, 225
  corruption, 162, 167, 170, 172–73, 177
  domestic policy, 4
  election of 1994, 1–2
  election of 2000, 2
  executive power, 194, 195, 197, 198, 199, 200
  Ford, Gerald, 86–87, 90
  Fox News, 131
  Haliburton, 61, 63, 85, 177
  Halloween Massacre, 86–87
  Hussein, Saddam, 62, 63
  Iraq War (1991), 62, 91, 116
  Iraq War (2003–), 92, 103, 104, 105, 116, 211

Lieberman, Joe, 61
McCain, John, 210
media and, 121–22, 123, 124
national security, 5
oil industry, 172–73
partisanship, 132–33
Powell, Colin, 62, 91, 94
power plays, 85–87
Republican national convention (1976), 18, 20
Republican Party and, 230
Rumsfeld, Donald, 77, 86–87, 89, 90, 92–94, 103
Torture Memo, 171
vice presidency, 81–85, 95–97
WMDs, 108–9
Cheney, Lynne, 1–2, 83–84
Chertoff, Michael, 185
ChoicePoint, 174
Christian Coalition, 25, 26, 48, 49, 156, 164
Churchill, Winston, 135
Civility, 213–21, 224
Civil War, 212
Clay, Henry, 14
Cleland, Max, 122, 123–24
Clemenceau, Georges, 103
Clinton, Hillary, 41, 50, 67, 104, 143, 200, 212, 230
Clinton, William Jefferson
Ailes, Roger, 129
Air Force One, 47
corruption, 161
family values, 50
Gingrich and 104th Congress, 12–13, 37, 39, 41, 45–46, 47, 48
Goldwater, Barry, 10–11
government shutdown and, 227
impeachment, 50, 52–53
Jackson, Andrew, 217
media and, 128
Medicare, 45–46
Neo-Cons and, 63, 100–101
presidential campaigning, 73, 75
religion, 26, 146
Rich, Marc, 95

symbolism, 182–84
U.S. military, 92
CNN, 108, 130
Coburn, Tom, 50
Colby, William, 88
Cold War, 20, 21, 208
Commanders, The (Woodward), 104
Congress Watch, 160
Connally, John, 68
Conscience of a Conservative, The (Goldwater), 216
Conservationist, 4, 172
Contraception, 30, 50
Contract with America, 36–37, 40, 49
Controlled Substances Act, 204
Coolidge, Calvin, 176, 217–18
Coors, Joseph, 23
Cornyn, John, 202–3
Corporatism, 4
Coulter, Ann, 122–23, 137, 192, 201
Court-packing plan, 201
"Cross of Gold" speech (Bryan), 48
Cuban Missile Crisis, 106
"Culture of life" issues. *See* Abortion; Euthanasia; *Roe v. Wade*; Schiavo, Terri; Stem-cell research
Cuomo, Mario, 2

D
Daley, Richard, 119
Darwin, Charles, 153
Daschle, Tom, 90
Daugherty, Harry, 175, 176
Death with Dignity Act, 203–4
Deaver, Mike, 24, 182
DeLay, Tom
Abramoff, Jack, 163
Boehner, John, 132
Clinton, William Jefferson, 12, 13, 52–53
Contract with America, 36, 49
corruption, 3, 43, 163, 227
judicial system and, 202–3
lobbyists, 43

religiosity of, 48, 49
Republican Party, 227, 230
Scanlon, Michael, 155, 163
Schiavo, Terri, 30, 148–49, 150, 152
Democratic National Committee, 134–35, 209
Democratic Party. *See individual Democrats*
Dewey, Thomas, 11–12
Dirksen, Everett, 140
Dobson, James, 156, 229
Dole, Bob, 19, 22, 38, 47, 68, 158
Doyle Dane Bernbach, 133–34
Dream Ticket, 18–19
Dred Scott, 201
Drew, Elizabeth, 39
Dubose, Lou, 52
Dukakis, Michael, 129
Dulles, John Foster, 106

E
Economics
Carter, Jimmy, 27
Goldwater, Barry, 4, 217
Hitler, Adolf, 193
Republican Party, 231
Rockefeller, Nelson, 87
Roosevelt, Franklin D., 128, 201
supply-side, 21, 231
Edwards, Lee, 210
Eisenhower, Dwight D., 48, 101
Elmer Gantry (Lewis), 192
Energy industry, 171–73
Euthanasia, 145, 203–4. *See also* Schiavo, Terri
Evangelicals. *See* Theo-Cons
Evolution, 152–54
Executive power
Bush administration, 193–97
Cheney, Dick, 199–200
Johnson, Lyndon B., 13
judiciary and, 201–4
Lewis, Sinclair, 191–93
Republican Party principles and, 231
Yoo, John, 197–200

F

Fabrizio, Tony, 23
Fact (magazine), 136
Fair Campaign Practices
    Committee (FCPC), 134–35
Fairfax Hotel, 10
Fairness Doctrine, 126, 128
Faith-based community, 22. *See
    also* Religious Right; Theo-
    Cons; *specific individuals*
Faith-based initiatives, 26, 193,
    216, 228
Fall, Albert, 175, 176
Falwell, Jerry
    Ashcroft, John, 156
    church and state, 25
    Goldwater, Barry, 5, 31, 206,
        207
    McCain John, 206–7, 210
    Moral Majority, 23, 25, 26, 31
    O'Connor, Sandra Day, 31, 201
    Republican national conven-
        tion (1980), 21
    Republican Party, 26, 229
Family planning, 25, 31, 50
Family Research Council, 143
Family values, 21, 31, 50, 95,
    185, 231
Federal Communications
    Commission (FCC), 126
Federal courts, 149, 152, 203. *See
    also* U.S. Supreme Court
Federal Emergency Management
    Agency (FEMA), 185
Federal Marriage Amendment, 181
Fiedler, Tom, 37
Fireside Chats, 128
Fitzgerald, Peter, 140
Flag Protection Amendment, 179,
    180–81
Flanigan, Timothy E., 170
Fleming, Thomas, 102
Focus on the Family, 156
Foley, Mark, 161
Foley, Tom, 56
Ford, Gerald
    Bush, George H. W., 68, 88

Cheney, Dick, 83, 86–87, 90,
    93
    Halloween Massacre, 86–87
    Republican national conven-
        tion (1980), 18, 19, 20, 69
    Rumsfeld, Donald, 60, 69, 93
Fox News, 2, 85, 125, 127, 130,
    131, 192
Free Congress Foundation, 23
Free-market economics, 4, 21, 46,
    217
Friedman, Milton, 231
Frist, Bill, 30, 147, 150, 179,
    180, 181
Frum, David, 111–15

G

Galileo, 154
Gardiner, Sam, 177
Gates, Robert, 76, 77
Gays in military, 10, 13, 22, 49,
    144
General Services Administration,
    166
Geneva Conventions, 171, 198
Gerson, Michael, 100, 111–15
Gingrich, Newt
    Air Force One, 47
    arrogance and vanity, 41–46
    Cheney, Dick, 82
    Clinton, William Jefferson, 37,
        39, 40–41, 45–46, 47, 48, 53
    Contract with America, 36–37,
        40, 49
    contradiction and hypocrisy,
        38–40
    election of 1994, 2
    Goldwater, Barry, 10, 11–12
    media and, 127–28
    Medicare, 46–47
    personal attacks, 37–38
    Starr, Kenneth, 50
Gingrich Revolution, 2, 11, 127.
    See also 104th Congress;
    Contract with America
Giuliani, Rudy, 229
Goldman, William, 8
Goldwater, Barry

Clinton, William Jefferson,
    10–11, 13
    conservatism, 3–5, 13, 15,
        164, 223, 224, 230
    Falwell, Jerry, 5, 31, 206, 207
    funeral, 234–35
    Gingrich revolution, 10–11,
        12, 13
    K Street, 175
    McCain, John, 205–7, 210–12
    media and, 135–36
    moral conservatism and, 22
    O'Connor, Sandra Day, 31
    political advertisements and,
        133–35, 137, 209
    political discourse, 212–21
    power and, 231
    presidential campaign and elec-
        tion (1964), 2, 5–6, 14,
        207–10, 232–34
    principles, 8–9, 207–10
    religious conservatism, 31–32,
        33, 48
    Republican Party and, 226
    symbolism and, 188–89
    Truman, Harry, 212
    Vietnam War, 205
    watchdog, 10
Goldwater, Morris, 213
Goldwater Doctrine, 211
Goldwaters of Arizona, The
    (Smith), 213
Gonzalez, Alberto, 5, 170–71,
    196–97, 198
Gore, Al, 2, 56, 61, 96, 158, 183
Government contracts
    Abramoff, Jack, 169
    Ashcroft, John, 174
    Haliburton, 4, 61, 63, 85,
        177, 187
    Hurricane Katrina, 187
    Iraq War, 85, 97, 177, 187
    lobbying and, 169, 174, 221
Government intrusion. *See* Theo-
    Cons
Government regulation, 36
Graham, Billy, 58
Grant, Ulysses S., 161, 195

Great Society, 6, 36, 149, 216
Greeley, Father Andrew, 145
Gregory, David, 167
Griles, J. Stephen, 171
Ground Zero, 183, 186
Gulf of Tonkin Resolution, 110, 210

H

Hagel, Chuck, 223, 225, 231
Hagin, Joe, 56
Haldeman, H. R., 97
Halliburton, 4, 61, 63, 85, 177, 187
Halloween Massacre, 86–87
Hamill, Pete, 3–4, 8, 13, 30, 213, 221, 235
Hammer Comes Down, The (Dubose and Reid), 52
Hannity, Sean, 128, 131
Harding, Warren G., 161, 175–76
HarperCollins, 42
Hart, Jeffrey, 224, 225
Hastert, Dennis, 3, 118, 150, 227, 230
Hatch, Orrin, 147, 180
Hawkins, George, 29
Hayakawa, Sam, 179–80
Hayek, F. A., 117
Health care program, 41
Hearst, William Randolph, 101
Hefley, Joel, 227
Heritage Foundation, 23
Hewitt, Hugh, 128
Hinckley, John, 80
Hitler, Adolf, 193, 195
Hodel, Donald, 25
Hollings, Fritz, 29
Homosexuality, 10, 13, 22, 49, 50, 144, 229
Hoover, Herbert, 218
House Government Reform Committee, 168
Hume, Brit, 131
Humphrey, Hubert, 28, 213
Hunger in America (documentary), 119

Hurricane Katrina, 30, 74, 166, 184–88
Hussein, Saddam
    bin Laden, Osama, 110
    Bush, George W., 90
    Iraq War (1991), 62, 91
    Neo-Cons and, 63, 91, 101
    Snow, Tony, 116
    WMDs, 105, 108, 109
Huxley, Aldous, 148

I

"If Grant had been Drunk at Appomattox" (Thurber), 212
"If the South had won the Civil War" (*Look* magazine article), 212
Illinois Senate race (2004), 139–43
Illusion of Victory, The (Fleming), 102
Impeachment
    Clinton, William Jefferson, 50, 52–53
    Nixon, Richard M., 125, 234
Influence peddling. *See* Lobbying
Intelligent Design, 152–54
Iran, 32, 112, 113–14, 216
Iran-Contra scandal, 51–52, 53
Iran-Contra scandal, 51–52, 53, 129, 130
Iraq War (1991)
    Bush, George H. W., 90–91, 102, 104–5, 115, 116
    Cheney, Dick, 61, 62, 91, 116
    Hussein, Saddam, 62, 91
    Powell, Colin, 61, 62, 104–5
Iraq War (2003–)
    Bush, George H. W., 66, 115–16
    Bush, George W., 58, 65, 90
    Chalabi, Ahmed, 195
    Cheney, Dick, 92, 103, 104, 105, 116, 211
    Haliburton, 85, 177
    historical analogies, 195–96
    Hurricane Katrina and, 187
    Hussein, Saddam, 90, 109, 113

invasion planning, 100–101, 103–4
    Libby, Scooter, 97
    McCain, John, 211
    media and, 121, 124
    midterm elections of 2006, 226–27
    Myers, Richard B., 185
    Ponnuru, Ramesh, 145
    Powell, Colin, 91, 94, 105–7
    propaganda campaign, 109–15
    Rice, Condoleezza, 107, 109, 110, 113, 115
    Rumsfeld, Donald, 77, 103
    Wehner, Peter, 194
    WMDs, 105, 107, 108–9, 109, 114
Irvin, Sam, 125
Isolationism, 4
Israel, 108–9
It Can't Happen Here (Lewis), 191–92, 193

J

Jackson, Andrew, 217
Jackson, Henry "Scoop," 6
Jackson, Jesse, 26
Jefferson, Thomas, 219
Jockey Club, 10, 11
Johnson, Lyndon B.
    executive power, 13
    Great Society, 36
    Gulf of Tonkin Resolution, 110, 210
    influence peddling, 175
    media and, 120
    political advertisements, 133–35, 137, 209
    political discourse, 214
    political vision, 230
    Vietnam War, 205
Jones, Chuck, 174
Judicial activism, 202,
Judiciary
    executive power and, 201–4
    Schiavo case, 149, 152, 203
    See also U.S. Supreme Court

K

Kasich, John, 36, 47, 48
Katrina. *See* Hurricane Katrina
Kendall, Willmoore, 224
Kennedy, Joe, 57
Kennedy, John F.
  Bush, George W., 93
  Goldwater, Barry, 214–15
  Kennedy, Joe, 57
  media and, 119
  party loyalty, 1
  religion, 48–49, 216
  Yale-Harvard ideologues, 111
Kennedy, Ted, 215
Kerry, John, 124
Kevorkian, Jack, 145
Keyes, Alan, 139–43
Kilpatrick, James J., 121, 127
Kirk, Russell, 38
Kissinger, Henry, 18, 20, 69, 106
Know-Nothings, 48
Koch, Ed, 8
Kondracke, Morton, 82
Korean War, 106
Kozlowski, Dennis, 170
Krauthammer, Charles, 108, 123
Kristol, Irving, 6, 7
Kristol, William, 7–8, 60, 63
Kristolites. *See* Neo-Cons
K Street Project, 118, 163. *See also* Lobbying
Kuo, David, 228, 229

L

Laffer, Arthur, 21, 231
Laissez-faire economics, 4
Language in Thought and Action (Hayakawa), 180, 181
Largent, Steve, 160
Laxalt, Paul, 69, 215
Lay, Ken, 161
Leach, Jim, 226
Leadership, 72–75
League of Nations, 102
Leahy, Pat, 85
Legal system, reform of, 36
Lewis, Sinclair, 191–93
Libby, I. Lewis "Scooter," 95, 97

Liberalism, 2, 6, 128
Libertarianism, 21, 22, 214, 217, 224
Liddy, Gordon, 125
Lieberman, Joe, 61
Limbaugh, Rush, 125, 127, 128, 137
Lincoln, Abraham, 219, 225
Lobbying
  Abramoff, Jack, 155, 161, 163–64, 165, 166–69, 171
  Agnew, Spiro, 118
  Ashcroft, John, 158, 159, 160, 173–74
  Bush administration, 160–61, 162, 165–73
  Cheney, Dick, 177
  Clinton administration, 161
  DeLay, Tom, 43, 163
  Goldwater, Barry, 221
  Haliburton, 177
  Harding, Warren G., 175–76
  Nixon administration, 162
  oil industry, 171–73
  Safavian, David, 166
  Scanlon, Michael, 155, 163–64
  U.S. House of Representatives and, 160, 162
  U.S. Senate and, 158–60
  See also Abramoff, Jack; Scanlon, Michael
Lodge, Henry Cabot, 102–3, 106
Long, Earl, 116
Long, Huey, 116, 192–93
Look (magazine), 212
Looking Forward (Bush), 65, 71, 92
Lott, Trent, 42, 184
Luntz, Frank, 49

M

MacArthur, Douglas, 193
Maddox, Lester, 29
Main Street (Lewis), 192
Making of a President, The (White), 217
Mann, James, 64, 99, 100, 103

Mann, Thomas, 73, 179
Marbury v. Madison, 201
McCain, John, 67, 104, 205–7, 210–12, 229
McClellan, Scott, 131
McComb, Phil, 83
McGovern, George, 6
McGrory, Mary, 107
McKinley, William, 102
McNamara, Robert, 9
Media
  Agnew, Spiro, 118–21, 122, 126, 127
  bloggers, 126
  Bush, George H. W., 67
  Bush, George W., 70, 74, 123–24, 132–33
  campaign coverage (1964), 135–37
  Cheney, Dick, 121–22, 123, 124
  Cleland, Max, 122, 123–24
  Coulter, Ann, 122–23
  Gingrich, Newt, 12, 42, 127
  Gingrich Revolution, 11
  Hannity, Sean, 128, 131
  Kerry, John, 124
  Limbaugh, Rush, 125, 127, 128, 137
  Limbaugh-Fox Revolution, 127–32
  lobbying scandals, 164
  Manichean, 127
  midterm elections (2002), 124
  Nixon administration and, 125–26
  O'Reilly, Bill, 125–26, 128, 192
  political advertising (1964), 133–35
  political party visibility and, 35
  radio, 128
  Rather, Dan, 129–30
  terrorism and, 124
  See also specific media outlets, newspapers, magazines, and related individuals
Medicare, 45–46

Meese, Ed, 20
Meyer, Frank, 224
Michels, Bob, 38, 140
Military-industrial complex, 101
Miller, Merle, 209
Mises, Ludwig von, 117
"Mission Accomplished" photo-op, 70, 115, 183
Missouri Senate race (2000), 155–58
Mitchell, George, 56, 158
Mondale, Walter, 96
Monroe, James, 219
Moral conservatism, 21–22, 23, 140. *See also* Religious Right; Theo-Cons; *individual moral conservatives*
Moralism, 4–5, 225. *See also* Theo-Cons
Moral Majority, 23, 24–25, 26, 31, 156
Mormons, 49
Morris, Dick, 44
Morton, Rogers, 88
Mossad, 109
MoveOn.org, 127
Moyers, Bill, 133–34, 135, 137, 209
Moynihan, Daniel Patrick, 106
Moynihan, Pat, 184–85
MSNBC, 121
Mundell, Robert, 21, 231
Murdoch, Rupert, 42, 43, 101, 126, 129, 130–32
Murrow, Edward R., 119
Myers, Julie, 185
Myers, Richard B., 185

N

National Council of Churches, 26
National defense, 36, 101
National Review, 126–27, 144
National Security Council, 59, 66, 107
Nation building, 38. *See also* Neo-Cons
Nazi Germany, 113, 196
NBC (television network), 120, 133, 167

Negroponte, John, 107
Neo-Cons, 6–8, 228, 229. *See also* Armitage, Richard; Cheney, Dick; Kristol, Irving; Kristol, William; Rice, Condoleezza; Rumsfeld, Donald; Wolfowitz, Paul; *other specific individuals*
New Deal, 36, 128, 201
New Orleans. *See* Hurricane Katrina
New Republic, 82
Newsweek (magazine), 58, 67, 120, 129, 234
New Yorker (magazine), 76, 86, 233
New York Herald Tribune, 119
New York Times, 82, 120, 121, 123, 136, 143, 147, 217, 228
Ney, Bob, 166
Nixon, Richard M.
  Agnew, Spiro, 118–19
  Bush, George H. W., 68
  Cheney, Dick, 86, 88
  corruption, 162
  Goldwater, Barry, 9, 234
  media and, 132
  Reagan, Ronald, 40
  Rumsfeld, Donald, 86, 88, 93–94
  United Nations, 106
  Vietnam War, 102, 106
  Watergate scandal, 68, 97, 125–26, 197, 234
Nofziger, Lyn, 19–20
Norquist, Grover, 12, 37, 168
North, Oliver, 129
North Atlantic Treaty Organization (NATO), 208
North Korea, 114
Norton, Gale, 171
Novak, Bob, 207, 233
Nuclear Test Ban Treaty, 134
Nunn, Sam, 93

O

Obama, Barack, 140, 141
O'Connor, Sandra Day, 31, 199, 201, 202, 206

Office of Economic Development, 86, 88
Office of Economic Opportunity, 94
Oil industry, 171–73
Olmstead v. U.S., 191
O'Neill, Tip, 37
Operation Scorpion, 91
Orben, Bob, 171
O'Reilly, Bill, 125–26, 128, 192
Ornstein, Norman, 73

P

Packwood, Bob, 158
Partial-birth abortion, 228
Party of Death, The (Ponnuru), 144
Pataki, George, 2
Patriotism, 50, 115, 180, 215
Patton, George, 220
Paxon, Bill, 36
Pearl Harbor, 113, 114, 132
Pentagon. *See* Neo-Cons; Rumsfeld, Donald; Wolfowitz, Paul
Perkins, Tony, 143
Perle, Richard, 63, 105
Permanent campaign, 73, 182
Photo-ops, 70, 74, 75, 115, 186, 189. *See also* Media
Pichot, Gifford, 172
Plame, Valerie, 97
Plant Food Institute, 28
Political ads, 133–35, 137, 209
Political compromise, 228–31
Political discourse, 212–21
Political divisiveness, 223–35
Ponnuru, Ramesh, 144, 145
Population control, 25
Pornography, 27
Powell, Alma, 99
Powell, Colin, 104–7
  Bush, George H. W., 59, 62, 66
  Bush, George W., 59, 63, 91
  Cheney, Dick, 61, 62, 63, 91, 92, 94
  Iraq War (1991), 61, 62, 104–5

Iraq War (2003–), 91, 94, 105–7

P-R as in President (Gold), 182

Prayer in schools, 21, 22, 25, 27, 49

Presidential leadership, 72–75

Principles, 8–9, 207–10

Privacy, 27

"Pro-choice," 28, 143–44

Prohibition, 49

Prohibition Party, 230

Project for a New American Century (PNAC), 63, 100–101

"Pro-life" issues. *See* Abortion; Euthanasia; *Roe v. Wade*; Schiavo, Terri; Stem-cell research

Propaganda. *See* Media

Protecting the Reference to God in the Pledge of Allegiance and National Motto Amendment, 181

Public Citizen, 160

Purdum, Todd, 56, 70

Q

Quayle, Dan, 64, 97

R

Rabin, Yitzhak, 47

Racism, 28–29

Radio, 128. *See also* Limbaugh, Rush; Media

Rainbow Coalition, 26

Ralston, Susan, 167–69

Rather, Dan, 129–30

Rayburn, Sam, 111

Reagan, Nancy, 20, 69

Reagan, Ronald
  bodyguards, 80
  Bush, George H. W., 68, 69
  conservatism and, 13, 15, 225, 230
  Coolidge, Calvin, 218
  Ford, Gerald, 87
  Gingrich, Newt, 40
  Goldwater, Barry, 6

Iran-Contra scandal, 51–52
  media and, 126
  Neo-Cons and, 7
  O'Connor, Sandra Day, 31
  religious conservatives, 24–25, 26
  Republican national convention (1980), 18–21
  Rumsfeld, Donald, 90
  symbolism, 24–25, 182

Reaganites, 21

Reagan's Revolution (Shirley), 19

Reed, Ralph, 48, 122, 164, 166, 229

Regime change. *See* Neo-Cons

Regulation, 36

Reid, Harry, 180

Reid, Jan, 52

Religiosity, 216–21

Religious conservatism. *See* Moral conservatism; Theo-Cons

Religious Right, 23, 32, 144, 156, 203, 226, 227, 228

Reno, Janet, 104

Republican Family Caucus, 50

Republican Governors' Conference (1964), 14

Republican National Committee, 156, 227–28

Republican national convention (1976), 20

Republican national convention (1980), 17–22, 69

Republican Party
  future of, 225–35
  resilience of, 14–15

Republican Party. *See also* Neo-Cons; Theo-Cons; *specific individuals*

Rhodes, John, 215

Rice, Condoleezza
  Bush, George H. W., 59
  Bush, George W., 59, 63
  Hussein, Saddam, 109
  Iraq War (2003–) buildup, 109, 110, 113, 115
  neoconservatism, 104, 107–8
  Vulcans, 99, 100

Rich, Marc, 95, 97

Richards, Ann, 2, 67, 70, 75, 129

Ridge, Tom, 174

Right Man, The (Frum), 111–15

Rise and Fall of the Third Reich, The (Shirer), 196

Rise of the Vulcans (Mann), 64, 99

Roberts, John, 204

Robertson, Pat
  Carter, Jimmy, 27
  Christian Coalition, 48, 156
  family values, 50
  moral conservatism, 23
  Republican national convention (1980), 21
  Republican Party, 26, 229

Rockefeller, Nelson, 19, 40, 86–87

Rockwell, Llewellyn H., Jr., 117, 122

Rodino, Peter, 125–26

Roe v. Wade, 27–28, 29, 143–44

Rogers, Will, 223

Rogers, William, 106

Rohrabacher, Dana, 165

Romney, Mitt, 49, 229

Roosevelt, Franklin D.
  Bush, George W., 93
  Gerson, Michael, 113
  Gingrich, Newt, 39
  Long, Huey, 192–93
  New Deal, 36, 128, 201
  political party system, 14
  radio, 128
  Reagan, Ronald, 24
  Supreme Court, 201

Roosevelt, Theodore, 14, 48, 171, 172, 217, 218, 219

Rosenthal, Andy, 82

Rostenkowski, Dan, 43, 163

Rove, Karl
  Bush, George W., 18, 59, 96
  Bush, Jeb, 76
  campaign strategy (2002), 123–24
  corruption, 167, 168–69, 171–72
  executive power, 194

partisanship, 32
political discourse, 214
Reed, Ralph, 122
Religious Right, 229
Republican Party, 3
Rumsfeld, Donald, 77
stem cell research, 145
symbolism, 183
Rovere, Richard, 233
Rumsfeld, Donald
Bush, George H. W., 77,
87–89, 92, 115
Bush, George W., 59–60, 76,
89, 92–94
Cheney, Dick, 60, 77, 85–87,
89, 90, 92–94, 103
executive power, 195
Ford, Gerald, 86
Fox News, 131
Gates, Robert, 76
Gingrich, Newt, 39
Halloween Massacre, 86–87
Iraq War, 211
media and, 124
Myers, Richard B., 185
partisanship, 132–33
regime change, push for, 63,
100, 103, 104, 105
Republican national conven-
tion (1980), 18–20, 69
Washington Post quote, 99
Rusk, Dean, 106
Ryan, Jim, 140

S
Safavian, David, 166–67
Safire, William, 50, 121, 127
Safire's New Political Dictionary
(Safire), 50, 51
St. Pé, Kerry, 187
Same-sex marriage, 144, 229
Sanders, Carl, 29
Scalia, Antonin, 204
Scanlon, Michael, 155, 163–64
Schiavo, Terri, 30, 144, 148–52,
202–3, 227
Schlesinger, Arthur, Jr., 102
Schlesinger, Arthur, Sr., 14, 102

School prayer, 21, 22, 25, 27, 49
Schorr, Daniel, 136
Scopes Trial, 153
Scowcroft, Brent, 62, 63, 86, 96,
97, 107
Segregation, 28–29
Sensationalism, of Gingrich, 44.
See also Media
Shirer, William L., 196
Shirley, Craig, 19
Simpson, Alan, 90
Smith, Chris, 50
Smith, Dean, 213
Snow, Tony, 115–16, 123, 131–32
Social conservatism, 23. *See also*
Moral conservatism
Solzhenitsyn, Alexander, 20
Specter, Arlen, 147, 200
Sperling, Godfrey, 46, 47
Starr, Kenneth, 13, 50, 53, 185
Starr Report, 53
State of the Union address
(2002), 81, 100, 111–15, 132
Stein, Herb, 21, 231
Stem cell research, 23, 30,
144–45, 146, 147–48
Stephanopoulos, George, 41
Stevenson, Adlai, 6, 106
Strict constructionists, 204
"Stupid Party, The" (Kristol), 7
Suez Crisis, 106
Sulzberger, C. L., 136
Sununu, John, 22
Supply-side economics, 21, 231
Symbolism
Federal Marriage Amendment,
181
Flag Protection Amendment,
179, 180–81
Goldwater, Barry, 188–89
Hayakawa, Sam, 179–80
politics of, 182–88
Protecting the Reference to
God in the Pledge of
Allegiance and National
Motto Amendment, 181
Reagan, Ronald, 24–25, 32

T
Taft, Robert, 202
Taft, William Howard, 14, 172
Talk radio, 128. *See also*
Limbaugh, Rush; Media
Tanner, Stephen, 66
Tauzin, Billy, 160
Taxes
Abramoff, Jack, 169
Contract with America, 36
faith-based initiatives and, 26,
216
Gingrich, Newt, 38
Hurricane Katrina photo-op,
74
Luntz, Frank, 49
Taylor, Guy, 196–97
Teapot Dome scandal, 165,
175–76
Teeter, Bob, 18
Televangelism, 21, 31. *See also*
Falwell, Jerry; Robertson, Pat;
Theo-Cons
Television media. *See* Media
Tenet, George, 105, 184
Term limits, 36
Terrorism
Ashcroft, John, 174
Boehner, John, 132
Bush, George W., 114
Cheney, Dick, 80
Gonzalez, Alberto, 197
Hitler, Adolf, 196
Keyes, Alan, 140
media and, 122, 124, 132
Myers, Julie, 185
scapegoating and, 186
symbolism and, 182
Yoo, John, 199
Theo-Cons, 139–54
Goldwater, Barry, 31–32
judiciary, 27–30, 31
Keyes, Alan, 139–43
political divisiveness and, 226,
227, 228, 229
Republican national conven-
tion (1980), 21–22
rise of, 22–27

Schiavo, Terri, 30, 144,
148–52, 202–3, 227
Wead, Doug, 32–33
See also Abortion; Euthanasia;
Intelligent Design;
Religious Right; Roe v.
Wade; Schiavo, Terri; Stem-
cell research; specific indi-
viduals
Third Wave, 38
Thomas, Clarence, 204
Thurber, James, 212
Time (magazine), 42, 120
Toffler, Alvin, 38
Toffler, Heidi, 38
Torture Memo, 170–71
Tower, John, 90
True Believers. See Theo-Cons
Truman, Harry, 11–12, 48, 175,
212, 213, 218–21
Tuohy, William, 234
Tyco International, 169–70, 171

U

Udall, Mo, 215
United Nations, 88, 106–7,
109
U.S. Civil War, 212
U.S. Department of Defense.
See Neo-Cons; Rumsfeld,
Donald; Wolfowitz, Paul
U.S. Department of Justice. See
Ashcroft, John; Gonzalez,
Alberto; Yoo, John
U.S. Forest Service, 172
U.S. Immigration and Customs
Enforcement Agency, 185
U.S. Supreme Court
Brown v. Topeka Board of
Education, 28, 29
executive power and, 201–4
judicial restraint, 204
Marbury v. Madison, 201
O'Connor, Sandra Day, 31,
199, 201, 202, 206
Olmstead v. U.S., 191
Roe v. Wade, 27–28, 29,
143–44

Roosevelt's court-packing plan,
201
Schiavo case, 203
Theo-Cons and, 27–30
Universal health care, 41
UPI (United Press International),
120
Uranium, enriched, 108, 109

V

Vietnam War, 39, 67, 106, 110,
115, 122, 205, 209, 210,
211–12
Vulcans, 99–100. See also
Armitage, Richard; Cheney,
Dick; Powell, Colin; Rice,
Condoleezza; Rumsfeld,
Donald; Wolfowitz, Paul

W

Walker, Bob, 36
Wallace, George, 28–29
Walsh, Lawrence, 53
War. See specific wars
Warner, John, 93
Warren, Earl, 29
Warren, Robert Penn, 192
Wars of the Bushes, The (Tanner),
66
Washington, George, 48, 102,
219
Washingtonian (magazine), 83, 84
Washington Post, 35, 82–83, 99,
120, 121, 123, 152, 160–61,
169, 199
Watergate scandal, 14, 68,
125–26, 197, 234
Watt, James, 25, 171
Wead, Doug, 32–33
Weapons of mass destruction
(WMDs)
Bush, George W., 90, 114
Cheney, Dick, 61, 108–9
Israel, 108
Neo-Cons, 104
Powell, Colin, 105, 107
Tenet, George, 184
UN inspectors, 67

Weaver, Richard, 38
Webster, Daniel, 193
Weekly Standard, 7, 60, 123, 131,
151
Wehner, Peter, 194–95
Weimar Constitution, 196
Weldman, Steven, 25
Welfare system, 36, 44, 49
We're Right, They're Wrong
(Carville and Begala), 127
Weyrich, Paul, 23–24, 49, 66,
229
White, Theodore, 14, 217
White House Office of Faith-
Based and Community
Initiatives, 32, 193, 228
Whitewater, 11
Whiz Kids, 9
Will, George, 121, 127, 194
Williams, Armstrong, 123
Willkie, Wendell, 146
Wilson, Woodrow, 7, 102–3
Wirthlin, Dick, 20
Wolfowitz, Paul, 9, 91, 93, 100,
104, 184
Woodward, Bob, 58, 63, 91, 104
World Bank, 184
World War II, 68, 113, 216
Wright, Jim, 37, 42

Y

Yarborough, Ralph, 69
"Yellow-cake" aluminum tubes,
109
Yoo, John, 197–200
Yoo Doctrine, 203